Brain Fitness
Puzzles

Also by Gareth Moore, PhD,
and Helena Gellersen, PhD

*Memory Palace Master: Over 70 Puzzles to Hone Your
Powers of Observation and Recall*

Brain Fitness
Puzzles

Stimulate Your Mind
with More Than 80 Exercises,
Games, and Tests

GARETH MOORE, PhD
HELENA GELLERSEN, PhD

Countryman Press

An Imprint of W. W. Norton & Company
Independent Publishers Since 1923

To all who helped me along the path
to becoming a scientist and most of
all to my family and Andrea.
I can't thank you enough!

– Helena Gellersen

Important Note to Readers

BRAIN FITNESS PUZZLES is intended for general informational and entertainment purposes only; it is not intended as medical advice or treatment. This book is sold without warranties of any kind, including warranties of fitness for any particular purpose, and none may be created or extended by sales representatives or promotional materials.

As of press time, any URLs displayed in this book link or refer to existing websites on the internet. Neither the publisher nor the authors may be held responsible for the accuracy, timeliness, or completeness of any content that appears on third-party websites.

Contents

INTRODUCTION

We humans have a remarkable capacity to learn, imagine, and reason, which has enabled our species to evolve from the first attempts to wield fire to the creation of the nuclear bomb within 300,000 years. To put that into perspective: if the Earth's age compressed from its 4.6 billion years to just 24 hours, we wouldn't appear until the last 90 seconds of the day—an impressively short period of time to become the dominant species on the planet.

The key to this success lies in that 3.3 pound fatty organ that uses up to 20 percent of the body's total energy consumption: the brain. The average human brain has about 86 billion neurons, which exchange trillions of signals with one another every second. Neuroscience only now is starting to uncover how the human brain can produce feats of art and science that shape our cultural history and our understanding of the world. Much remains that scientists don't understand yet. But learning, creative thinking, and reasoning are inherently human, meaning that every one of us has the basic machinery required for these abilities. Even better: you can learn how to use this machinery more effectively.

What Will This Book Do?

In this book, you'll read about the basics of the brain and key players in human cognition that keep us going in our endeavors to remember, learn, solve problems, and think creatively. You'll go from theory to practice as you tackle increasingly challenging puzzles that cover a variety of cognitive functions.

Before you embark on this journey, keep in mind that science can't offer a magic wand that you can wave or a spell book that will teach you magically how to boost your brain power. Just as your body grows gradually stronger as you run or lift weights, your brain also needs time to change. Completing mental exercises won't transform you into the next Einstein. But science can give you the knowledge of how the brain executes its various cognitive functions to help you add to the repertoire of strategies that you can use to complete these exercises more efficiently and carry your knowledge into everyday life.

Why Should I Care?

Health professionals and the general public long have focused on physical health. Brain health has become a hot topic only more recently. Of course, these two concepts link together: what's good for your muscles, your cardiovascular system, and your gut is also good for your brain. They all connect, after all. Some exercises might not make you sweat in the literal sense but will flex your brain. Keeping cognitively active and challenging yourself with new tasks and experiences lie at the core of a healthy brain. View this book as one part of a toolkit to keep handy when you feel like it's time for some mental exercise and when you want to learn more about the organ that holds the secrets to your memories, your intelligence, and your creativity.

Learning means acquiring new knowledge and skills, thereby improving your existing capabilities. When done right, it also provides other powerful psychological benefits. You may have heard that physical exercise can release biochemicals that improve mood and reduce stress. Intriguingly, though, you may not have to don gym clothes to achieve similar effects. Mental exercises and learning also can prove deeply satisfying when providing engaging challenges, such as the puzzles in this book.

We humans have a natural curiosity, which has helped ensure our survival and evolution. It drove us to venture into new territory, discover new species of plants and animals, test the boundaries of our abilities, and devise new uses for materials around us. Without the need for discovery and a hunger for learning, we never would have come to where we stand today. The journey of learning therefore can serve as its own reward.

Varied Practice

Similar to any physical exercise, variety is also key for mental fitness. Completing a thousand sudoku or hundreds of crossword puzzles may feel fun and relaxing—and there's nothing wrong with that, of course—but if you're looking for a little more, then getting outside your comfort zone matters. Your brain is inherently curious, but it also gets lazy. Just as curiosity had an important evolutionary benefit, this "laziness" reflects a different, powerful evolutionary mechanism: the brain's ability to establish routines that minimize the effort needed to function effectively.

Completing the same, familiar exercise repeatedly feels comfortable because you know what to expect, you know what to do, and you know that you will succeed. If you're a sudoku pro or a crossword mastermind, this positive expectation means that completing the exercise will feel rewarding. You are exploiting your existing cognitive resources. This is great when you begin a new exercise session because it will help you feel comfortable and familiar with it. However, the mental energy expended on a familiar task may be minimal, and your brain doesn't need to develop new resources or learn new strategies to expand your knowledge and skills. This is where the benefit of exploring tasks with novel demands helps, even if it may feel daunting at the beginning.

This choice between exploration, or curiosity-driven behavior, and exploitation, or the tendency to choose a safer bet, is ubiquitous in everyday life. Think about the last time you went to your favorite restaurant and had to decide whether to have a tried-and-tested usual or a new option on the menu. If you're confronted with particularly challenging tasks that may feel discouraging as you work your way through this book, remember that you're pushing your brain to explore, which ultimately gives you the key to expanding your mental resources and will help get you out of a routine.

The Cognitive Battery

Most details in life are fleeting: the words spoken by a friend during a dinner conversation, the images flickering before you while watching a movie—they're here in an instant and then gone. But we need to hold on to them to keep track of the conversation, the plot of the movie, or this very sentence. Otherwise, we would lose any sense of context and perpetually find ourselves in a state of confusion.

The first challenge for your brain therefore is to retain information even after it's no longer present in the environment. However, not everything we see, hear, or smell is relevant at a given point in time. When you're focusing on the conversation with your friend, you don't need to hear what the couple at the neighboring table is discussing (even if it feels tempting to listen).

Another challenge for your brain is to block out distractions not crucial for the task at hand, while making sure that you're still capable of responding to other potentially important information, for instance when your phone rings unexpectedly or someone nearby calls out your name. This complex feat requires cognitive flexibility to direct your limited attentional capacities to relevant information and adapt quickly to new task demands.

These functions form the bedrock for many complex cognitive tasks, as you'll see. One type of puzzle you'll encounter in this book aims to teach you strategies to retain more information in your short-term memory and use it flexibly to solve complex problems.

We rely on our sense of vision most and have a dedicated short-term memory system for visuospatial stimuli separate from the one in which we store verbal information. This visual system helps us to form correct representations of objects and their relationships, which in turn helps us to manipulate the world around us to fit our needs. One popular exercise for this type of task is the Rubik's Cube, in which you have to move differently colored square tiles on a cube so all squares of the same color appear on one side of the cube. While you may not break the speed record in a puzzle cube competition after reading this book, the puzzles that target visuospatial cognition will challenge you to manipulate visual information in your mind's eye better.

Besides short-term memory, your brain also has long-term memory systems that ensure that you can recall information you experience in your environment at a later time, enabling you to remember that dinner conversation the next time you see your friend, bringing to mind cherished moments of your last vacation, reciting the lyrics to a favorite song, or acing an exam. Certain strategies can help you increase the likelihood of making newly learned information available, at a later time, and in this book you'll have the opportunity to try your hand at some of them.

The most high-level human cognitive functions involve creativity and reasoning. These abilities have given rise to humankind's greatest accomplishments: art and culture that have endured for centuries and even millennia; inventions of technologies that allow us to shape the world around us; and great discoveries that give us a deeper understanding of the universe, whether of planets light-years in the distance or cells in the organ that allow you to comprehend this sentence. Becoming the next da Vinci requires a lifetime of disciplined study (in addition to what was likely an unfair genetic advantage). But you can hone your creative and logical thinking skills one step at a time by learning more about the processes that support you in solving complex problems and avoiding common pitfalls.

Your Journey

After any intense physical exercise, ending with a restorative stretch and cool-down is essential. For your mental exercises, finishing with some simpler puzzles will keep you from getting too discouraged if the higher-difficulty exercises felt overly frustrating at times or if you found it difficult to progress.

In this book, you can test yourself on a variety of cognitive skills, including exercises that tax your memory, your mental flexibility, your visuospatial skills, your reasoning, and your creative thinking. That diversity presents novel challenges at each turn of a page, giving you the opportunity to benefit from a wide variety of exercises. It also gives you an understanding of where your strengths lie and where you might benefit most from focusing your attention when attempting new puzzles.

The structure of this book imitates a physical exercise session, with a warm-up, strength training, a high-intensity "cardio" challenge, and a cool-down. No successful exercise begins with the heaviest weights or the fastest speed. Similarly, when taking on the puzzles in this book and trying your hand at new strategies, you may want to get in the groove with something light to warm up. You can begin comfortably with puzzles that feel familiar, that get your creative juices flowing, and that prepare you for the next level. You gradually will face more challenging puzzles that build on your learning from previous sections. You also will read about strategies that you can employ to become more proficient at the exercises.

Mix It Up

Through this journey, set your own pace and develop your own structure of how to approach these tasks. If on a given day you prefer to keep it light, go with some warm-up exercises and a few puzzles from the second difficulty level. If you feel like it's time for a challenge, warm up and then jump to the high-intensity puzzles. Learning should feel fun and rewarding yet challenging enough not to become discouraging. To keep you motivated and keep track of your progress, each puzzle awards you with a number of points, depending on how successfully you complete the exercise—see **Track Your Points** (page 190) for further information. Note the number of points you earn per page by using the points boxes at the top of the relevant pages, then review and compare your achievements on subsequent sessions.

Pesky Habits

It's hard to shake a bad habit, and it can prove just as hard to establish new ones. Anyone who ever started a diet, a new workout routine, or a new reading program can attest to that. If some habits keep us from achieving our goals, why would nature devise such a seemingly flawed system? It's easy. Habits don't require many cognitive resources, meaning that you don't have to think much. When you're trying to quit junk food, your brain automatically will send you to the ice cream in the freezer.

Ironically, when you want to learn something new, you want exactly that automatization. Cognitive training establishes new routines that allow you to solve problems more efficiently. That efficiency excels when you've internalized strategies, automated the cognitive machinery needed to solve a task, and, as a result, increased processing speed for similar tasks. The automatic craving for ice cream is the price that we all pay for the effortless use of language and ease of doing basic arithmetic. When you're trying to break or make a habit, it's helpful to change your environment in a way that makes the habit harder to follow (placing the jar of cookies at the back of the top shelf) or easier to start (having your workout clothes or puzzle book within easy reach).

To help form a routine for your cognitive training, develop a strategy for how you want to work through this book. Do you want to make steady progress and follow a strict routine, or do you prefer to take it easy? Do you set aside a certain amount of time every day? Do you want to set a certain time of day as your dedicated puzzle time? There's nothing wrong with going with the flow and deciding spontaneously—it all depends on what you want to achieve. But studies have shown that, for both physical and mental exercises, setting a specific goal and schedule at the get-go can help to keep you going in the longer term. So does rewarding yourself after you've completed your exercises. Just make sure that the reward doesn't outweigh the mental effort you exerted to complete the puzzles. Your favorite dessert for a completed sudoku or reasoning puzzle may be a bit too generous.

Support Brain Health

A healthy brain has many building blocks, giving you plenty of ways to take your health into your own hands. Here are some of the best, scientifically proven steps that you can take to help maintain and even improve cognitive function.

The first tool in your arsenal is what you're holding now: a means to promote lifelong learning and cognitive engagement. As you know, novelty and diverse experiences keep your brain from sliding into lazy routines. For instance, occupations that require managing people, analyzing data, operating complex machinery, or completing projects with varying requirements already provide substantial benefits by providing new challenges day by day. If you're enjoying retirement, it's important to replace such experiences with other means of challenging your brain. Excellent leisure-time examples include learning a new language, playing musical instruments, engaging in other artistic pastimes, or taking up a hobby that requires new motor skills, such as dancing, tennis, or golf.

Physical activity and diet importantly support health, and with good reason. Exercise improves heart, lung, and muscle function, benefits memory and cognitive abilities, promotes the growth of new blood vessels in the brain, and even results in new neurons in some brain regions. But you don't have to start practicing for a marathon just yet. High-intensity exercise most effectively promotes these positive effects on the brain, but even walking for half an hour brings benefits versus prolonged sitting. A varied diet full of vitamin-rich fruit and vegetables and healthy fats—such as those in nuts, certain types of oils, and fish—also forms the basis of a healthy body and brain.

It may surprise you to learn that social engagement matters just as much as healthy behavior. It seems so simple, yet maintaining a healthy social network and interacting with different people help the brain because those complex tasks involve exposure to novelty and the processing and memorization of information about many individuals and their relationships. Even more importantly, social engagement protects people from experiencing loneliness, one of the most detrimental factors to mental and cognitive health, given the deep-rooted human need for connection and belonging.

Good sleep also keeps us healthy, with most people requiring about 7 to 8 hours every night. Much about the role of sleep still remains an enigma, but we know that during sleep the brain promotes the formation of permanent new connections among cells necessary for learning, a process called neuronal plasticity. Scientists think that it's one of the reasons that newborns spend most of their time sleeping. Severe sleep deprivation can kill, and a chronic lack of sleep or poor sleep quality not only will affect mood and energy levels, but it also will slow the brain, impede the formation of new memories, and increase the risk of cognitive decline. Ultimately, poor sleep will make it more difficult to exercise or to eat healthily. It also will make it less likely that you'll reap the benefits from completing the puzzles in this book. So make sure to get some good rest!

There's no such thing as the holy grail for a healthy brain. Rather, a *fit* brain consists of multiple smaller pieces. The more of these healthy behaviors you do, the better, but of course it's not always easy to tick every box. Most people juggle many responsibilities. Education, jobs, caring for others, stressing about adhering to all the health advice that you receive, all of it can degrade your health because it can create anxiety. Take the steps that you can and gradually but continuously begin to work on incorporating others. As you know, building new habits is difficult, and if you hope to make lasting changes, small accomplishments will take you further than large expectations of immediate, life-changing effects, which ultimately may leave you feeling disappointed and make you more likely to quit. That goes for the puzzles in this book and the other health behaviors described here.

You've learned quite a bit about the basics of a healthy brain and key cognitive functions, but you're only getting started. So let's dive into practice and begin your puzzle journey.

Good luck!

1.
WARM UP

New challenges can feel daunting, so we'll start slowly and gradually increase the difficulty of the exercises to get you in the right groove. In this chapter, you'll learn about some basic concepts of how the brain supports core cognitive functions, and you'll try your hand at a variety of puzzles geared to tax each of them. But before you start, take some time to think about what you hope to gain from your journey through this book.

A Good Team

Any good team needs diversity, effective division of labor, and communication. After all, you want to create synergy. At the same time, it's also important to avoid total breakdown if one member of the team underperforms, sustains injury, or leaves entirely. The same goes for your means of communication. To remain robust, your team members and their possible communication channels need flexibility and some redundancy of skills. The brain balances these needs quite well. Certain regions specialize in particular cognitive functions such as vision, hearing, planning, and creating new memories, but they don't work alone. Cells can rewire themselves and do the jobs of their neighbors to some extent. That's why, in the course of Alzheimer's disease, for example, neurodegeneration can occur before a person notices cognitive decline.

Once we reach adulthood, most brain regions cease to generate new neurons. In adults, it's not so much the number of new neurons that reflects how much we have learned or can. The tree-shaped neurons already have settled comfortably within their forest of cells, and they won't go anywhere. Instead, what changes are the branch-like appendages with which the cell stretches toward its neighbors to pass along information. Learning can result in the formation of new or altered connections among cells and brain regions. You can liken this result to your team of neurons improving at processing information and communicating more successfully with one another to master a task.

Researchers call these changes brain plasticity, meaning our remarkable capacity for learning that we maintain even into older age. That's also why it's possible to bounce back from cognitive impairment observed right after a traumatic brain injury or stroke. As a goal, you'll be pursuing the formation of new connections and making them last, reflecting your improved skills and acquired knowledge. Your gray matter can't go for a run, but the cells within it sure can move to form new branches and therefore new connections.

Now let's meet the members of your team that you'll send through the exercises in this book.

Your Note Taker: Short-Term Memory

Just seeing the environment can't guide action effectively. Visuospatial information, speech, taste, and smell can disappear quickly from our surroundings, and, to act on them, we need some form of representation even after their physical presence has ceased. Our brain has dedicated, short-term memory storage mechanisms that act as a buffer to keep in mind just-experienced information even after it has disappeared from the immediate environment. Rather than letting it slip away like sand through a sieve, the brain regions that process auditory input can maintain something akin to an echo of this information, while the brain regions responsible for vision do the same with visual stimuli. However, these extremely vulnerable echoes fade quickly if not immediately relevant to our actions and if we don't focus our attention to hold on to them. Essentially, your short-term storage acts like a note taker with only a blackboard available to jot down a flood of new information. Once the board is full, the note taker needs to wipe the board to keep up, and not everything written there will survive the process. Too much interference from subsequent stimuli degrades the contents of your buffer.

In its most basic form, short-term memory simply holds information in mind just as you experienced it. You can practice that ability in the following puzzle.

1.1 Digit Memorization

Read through the first line of digits below just once. Then cover this page and write the digits as accurately as you can remember on the opposite page. Repeat with each line on this page until you no longer can repeat the full line of digits correctly. This task will give you an idea of the natural limits of your short-term memory.

Line 1

8 2 7 4 3 7

Line 2

7 3 5 1 2 4 5

Line 3

4 0 9 2 4 3 0 1

Line 4

8 1 4 0 5 2 6 3 9

Line 5

3 6 4 1 5 8 2 4 7 2

Line 6

5 9 3 1 8 2 0 7 3 6 4

POINTS

Recall

Line 1

....

Line 2

....

Line 3

....

Line 4

....

Line 5

....

Line 6

....

Your Architect: Working Memory and Executive Functions

As you go through life, you don't need to keep just an echo or reflection of the stimuli around you in your mind. You also need to use these representations to plan actions and make decisions. Note taking on its own doesn't work when you need to manipulate the contents of your short-term memory to meet a goal. Researchers have termed active manipulation of short-term storage as working memory. Think of it as short-term memory in action.

Working memory belongs to a set of processes that control and guide our thoughts and actions: executive functions, which serve as the architect of cognition. They take the building blocks in your short-term memory storage, plan steps to achieve a goal defined by the task at hand, help in the active search of your long-term memory to find the knowledge needed to complete that task, inhibit unsuitable options, monitor your progress as you approach your goal, and update your status as you work your way through a problem.

Sounds a little complicated and abstract, right? Let's take a look at puzzle **1.2 Country Confusion** (page 32) in which you have to rearrange the letters of words to form names of countries. In this word puzzle, you need to manipulate visual short-term memory representations to move around the individual elements. It's relatively simple for the first word:

few letters need to move, there are few possible solutions.
But it becomes more challenging as the words become longer.
You need to remember more elements, you need to retrieve
more potential options from long-term memory, you need to
put aside incorrect possibilities, and you need to make sure
you aren't missing any letters. The puzzles in this book will
focus on working memory to train not only your short-term
storage capacity but also your cognitive flexibility.

1.2 Country Confusion

Unscramble the names of each of these countries. Each country name is a single word, so ignore any spaces in the anagrams.

PURE

TANGO

SERIAL

REGALIA

OR YAWN

ROAD CUE

POLAR GUT

TAN REGINA

O ROMANCE

LIZARD NEWTS

Your Architect (continued)

As you can see, executive functions form the bedrock of deliberate, complex conscious functions and are ubiquitous across domains of human cognition. Some neuroscientists regard them as the pinnacle of our cognitive evolution and key to intelligence.

When tackling new and complex tasks, your architect must learn the inner workings of how best to complete an exercise. As you become more proficient and accustomed to the approach that a puzzle requires, your processing speed will increase. Whether you complete the grid in **1.3 Sudoku 6×6** (page 34), find your way to Paris in **1.5 Travel Network** (page 36), find complex patterns in **1.6 Odd One Out** (page 37), or think creatively with **1.17 What's in the Box?** (page 55), executive functions have you covered.

1.3 Sudoku 6×6

Complete each of these sudoku puzzles by placing a numeral from 1 to 6 into each empty square so that no digit repeats in any row, column, or bold-lined 3×2 box.

	3				5
2					
		6		2	
	4		5		
					2
4				6	

			6		1
			5		
4				6	
	1				4
		2			
5		3			

1.4 Dominoes

Draw along the dotted lines to divide each grid into a complete set of dominoes, from 0-0 to 4-4. Each domino will appear exactly once, so use the cross-off charts to keep track of which dominoes you've placed.

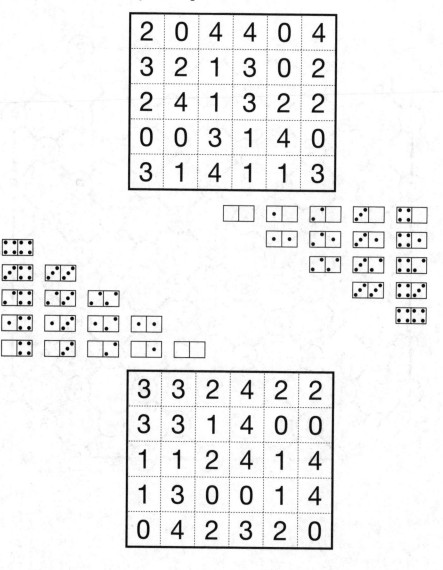

1.5 Travel Network

Can you find your way to PARIS in this network? Start on any circle and follow the lines to connected circles so that five circles connected in any combination of directions spell PARIS. No circle can be revisited.

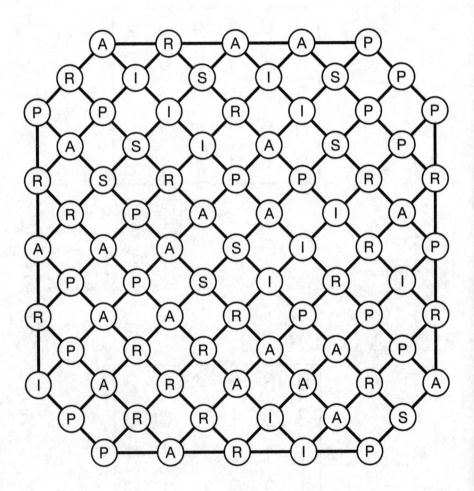

1.6 Odd One Out

Which of the images, A to E, is the odd one out from each set and why?

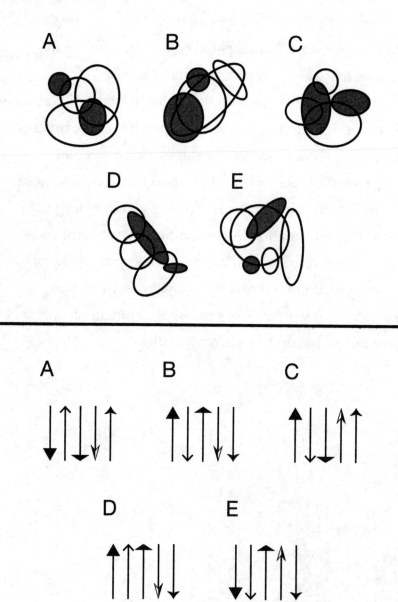

Your Sketch Pad: Visuospatial Cognition

To navigate the environment, the brain needs to represent the spatial relationships among objects and people to prevent you from bumping into them, reaching into empty space when trying to grab that apple on the table, or getting lost in the grocery store. Visuospatial cognition refers to the processes that help us tackle these challenges.

Including three-dimensional puzzles in a two-dimensional book poses a challenge. But you can practice a few functions of visuospatial cognition on the page, such as mental rotation. Mental rotation and reflection tasks such as those in **1.7 Reflect on This** (page 39) require you to manipulate visuospatial information in your mind's eye to form an internal, three-dimensional image of a complex object or environment. If you've read the previous section, you already can guess that these visuospatial functions intricately intertwine with working memory abilities.

1.7 Reflect on This

Imagine reflecting each of these two images in the dashed lines shown. Which lower image, A to D, then results in each case? Ignore the changes in scale.

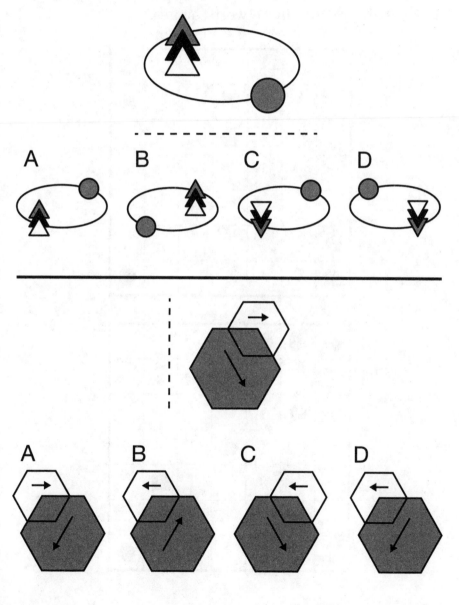

1.8 Shape Link

In each of the two puzzles below, draw a series of separate paths that each connects a pair of identical shapes. No more than one path can enter any square, and paths can travel only horizontally or vertically between squares.

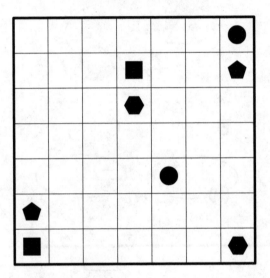

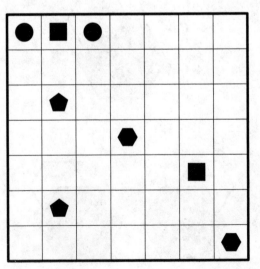

1.9 Top-Down Problem

Which of the options, A to D, represents the view of each 3D object when seen from the direction of the arrow?

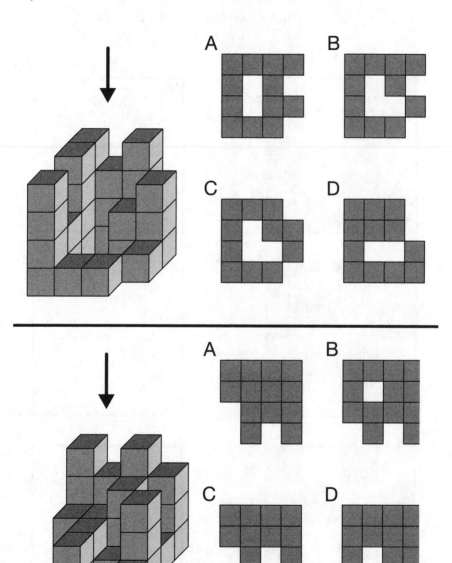

1.10 Grid Memory

Study the pattern in the first grid on the left of the page, then cover it and try to reproduce it accurately in the empty grid to the right. Repeat for the second and third grids.

 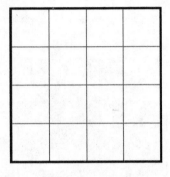

 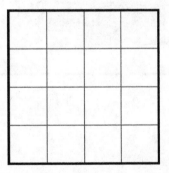

 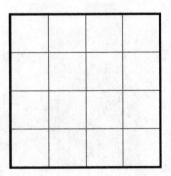

1.11 Building Blocks

In each of the puzzles below, which set of blocks, A to D, can rearrange to form the assembly shown? All blocks must be used exactly once each.

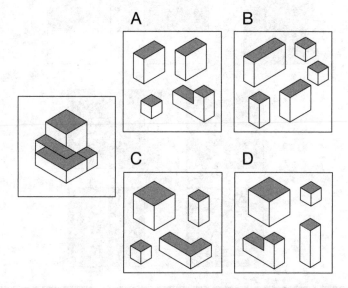

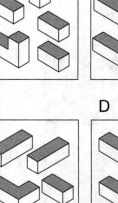

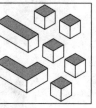

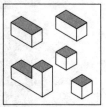

1.12 Fold and Punch

Imagine folding and then punching paper as shown in each of the two puzzles. Unfold, and which image, A to D, results?

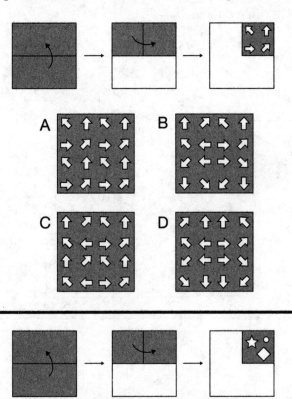

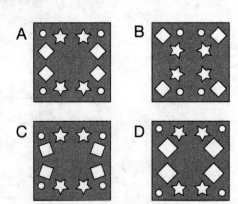

Your Sketch Pad (continued)

Becoming better at forming and manipulating mental images can help with a variety of other functions, such as using certain memory strategies to recall information more easily. Interestingly, better visuospatial abilities often facilitate learning even complex scientific concepts. For instance:

▶ for a chemist, imagining the arrangement of different elements in a molecule can benefit remembering how different substances may react with one another;

▶ in engineering, mentally assembling different pieces to form a new design is crucial;

▶ and a surgeon requires an excellent mental 3D model of a patient's anatomy to make the right cut.

Your Librarian: Long-Term Memory

Learning requires storing information for the long haul. The more you know, the more you can draw on existing knowledge and use it to solve problems, for instance by combining different pieces of information to arrive at novel conclusions and solutions. Long-term memory has a remarkable capacity: language, facts, motor skills, autobiographical memories, they all live within those billions of cells.

But most of what we experience every day never makes it into our permanent library. Why do we forget so much? Researchers have posited that our memory systems didn't evolve to take snapshots of our world or keep a detailed journal. Doing so would take up a lot of resources and our survival simply didn't depend on that. It did depend on:

▶ learning new motor skills

   (*Throw that spear!*);

▶ accurate and fast categorization of objects, contexts, and living beings

   (*Is that a tiger? Can I eat that berry?*);

▶ recall of inter-group relationships

   (*Can I trust that group member, or will they try to steal my food? Who in this group gets along well; who doesn't?*);

▶ successful communication

   (*I run ahead, and you two go left and right to cut off our prey's escape routes!*);

▶ and the use of all this knowledge to plan ahead

   (*I shouldn't take those two on a hunting party because they don't work well together, so I'll take the one who is the better spear thrower*).

If you look at it from that perspective, your long-term memory does an excellent job. Nevertheless, it does get frustrating to ask people for their names again or having to search for your password because you don't recall it by heart. In the following chapters, you'll learn some helpful mnemonic strategies. For now, warm up with **1.13 Password Posers** (page 48).

1.13 Password Posers

Cover the questions below the dividing line, then spend up to 1 minute memorizing these four codes and passwords. Once time is up, reveal the questions beneath.

Bank card PIN: **3971**
Email password: **D14MoND**
Alarm passcode: **468123**
Work password: **o1f2f3i4c5e**

Recall

Cover the top part of the page and see if you can answer the following questions:

1. What is the bank card PIN?
2. What word does the email password spell out, swapping digits for similar-looking letters?
3. What six-letter word lies within the Work password, alternating with the digits?
4. Which digit appears in all four passwords?
5. If you add together the six digits in the alarm passcode, what's the total?
6. Which code or password contains only odd digits?

1.14 F Is for (Not) Forgetting

Cover everything beneath the dividing line on this page. Study this list of animals until you think you've memorized it completely. Once you're ready, cover the list and reveal the instructions below the divider.

Fox
Frog
Fossa
Ferret
Firefly
Flamingo

Recall

Rewrite the list, writing the animal names in the same order. The spaces below indicate how many letters each name contains.

1.15 A Grimm Story

Cover the text on the opposite page. Now read the following text, abridged from *Grimms' Fairy Tales,* a few times until you think you remember the phrasing used. Then continue opposite.

"A king and queen once upon a time reigned in a country where there were in those days fairies. This king and queen had plenty of money, plenty of fine clothes to wear, and plenty of good things to eat and drink; but though they had been married many years, they had no children, which grieved them very much indeed.

One day, as the queen was walking by the side of the river, she saw a poor little fish that had thrown itself from the water and lay gasping and nearly dead on the bank. The queen took pity on the little fish and threw it back again into the river; and before it swam away it lifted its head from the water and said, "I know what your wish is, and it shall be fulfilled, in return for your kindness to me, you soon will have a daughter." What the little fish foretold soon came to pass; and the queen had a little girl so very beautiful that the king could not cease looking on it for joy.

Recall

Now cover the opposite page. The text below is almost identical to the original you just memorized, except that ten of the words in the passage have changed. Which ten words, and can you remember what they were before?

A king and queen once upon a time reigned in a citadel where there were in those days pixies. This king and queen had plenty of money, plenty of ridiculous clothes to wear, and plenty of good things to eat and drink; but though they had been married twenty years, they had no children, which annoyed them very much indeed.

One day, as the queen was walking by the side of the river, she saw a poor little fish that had thrown itself from the water and lay giggling and nearly dead on the bank. The queen took pity on the hilarious fish and threw it back again into the waterfall; and before it swam away it lifted its head from the water and said, "I know what your wish is, and it shall be fulfilled. In return for your kindness to me, you soon will have a son." What the little fish foretold soon came to pass, and the queen had a little boy so very beautiful that the king could not cease looking on it for joy.

1.16 Grocery Genius

Cover everything beneath the dividing line on this page. Then study this list of groceries until you think you've memorized it completely. Once you're ready, cover the list and reveal the instructions below the divider.

Apples   **Eggs**
Bananas   **Flatbread**
Carrots   **Grapes**
Donuts   **Halloumi**

Recall

Rewrite the list of items in the same order. The first letter of each item appears below to help you.

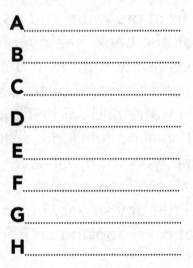

A..

B..

C..

D..

E..

F..

G..

H..

Your Out-of-the-Box Thinker: Creative Problem Solving

Around 3 million years ago, *homo habilis,* one of our close evolutionary ancestors, came up with unusual uses for common objects in the environment, fashioning them into tools. This development represented a huge feat of creative thinking: the ability to imagine a desired outcome and novel solutions.

Of course, human creativity does not produce only practical solutions to the problems we face, it also generates works of art that we find aesthetically pleasing. Almost every known culture has works of art, suggesting that creativity may serve as an inherent property of our brain. Being creative provided our evolutionary ancestors with an edge over the competition as humans faced a variety of complex challenges in the struggle to survive.

Increasing your creativity to produce beautiful, aesthetic works of art is a worthwhile goal in its own right, but it has less to do with puzzles. This book focuses on exercises known to promote creative thinking in a way that allows for new approaches to problems. This process, called lateral thinking, stands separate from traditional logical thinking and reasoning because it may not derive from a step-by-step approach using all available evidence within a given problem. Essentially, creativity allows for out-of-the-box thinking.

Get your creative juices going by thinking about **1.17 What's in the Box?** (page 55) and then what's outside it in **1.18 Object-ive Thinking** (page 56).

1.17 What's in the Box?

In this creativity challenge, draw in the boxes what you think lies inside them.

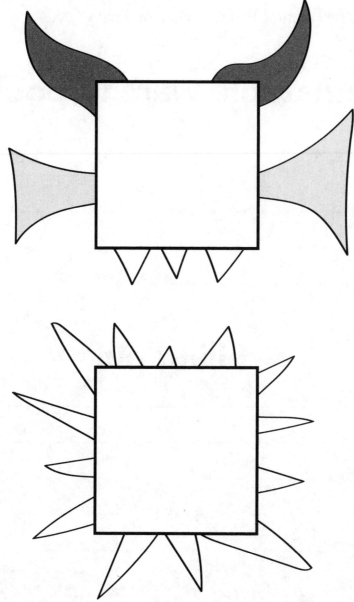

1.18 Object-ive Thinking

How many unusual uses does each of the objects listed below have? Write down as many as you can think of and avoid including anything that the object "normally" does.

inflatable wading pool

....

....

....

....

rolling pin

....

....

....

....

Your Logician: Reasoning Skills

Reasoning involves using information to arrive at logical conclusions. Using logical thinking, you can discover regularities in the world to make predictions about what will happen in the future and to plan ways to achieve your goals. Scientists who study the evolution of early humans and our biological ancestors have suggested that living in social groups, in which coordinated action led to our survival, helped develop our reasoning skills. But what constitutes logical reasoning? There are different types. For instance, you may receive a rule that you know to be true and that you then apply to solve a given problem. Take sudoku: the rules are defined clearly. All you have to do is follow them to solve the puzzle, such as with **1.3 Sudoku 6×6** (page 34). Common problems of arithmetic require these types of reasoning skills, though sudoku itself doesn't involve any pure mathematical deductions because the digits act as symbols.

1.19 Number Pyramid

Write a number in each empty block so that every block
(above the bottom level) equals the sum of the two blocks
directly beneath it.

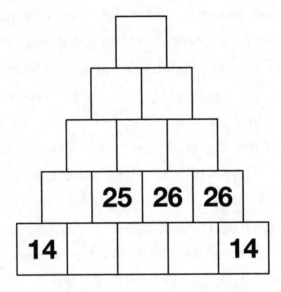

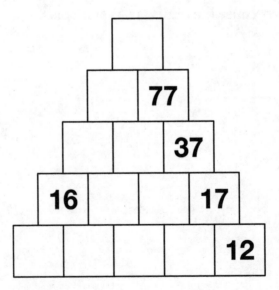

1.20 Food Swap

Cover the bottom half of this page, then spend a minute or two studying this set of food-related images. Once you're ready, cover them and read below.

Recall

Now cover the top half of the page. Circle the images below that are new and didn't appear above.

1.21 What's Missing?

The eight boxes below contain eight steps in a logical sequence now jumbled out of order. One of the boxes is empty, however. Draw the correct picture in it.

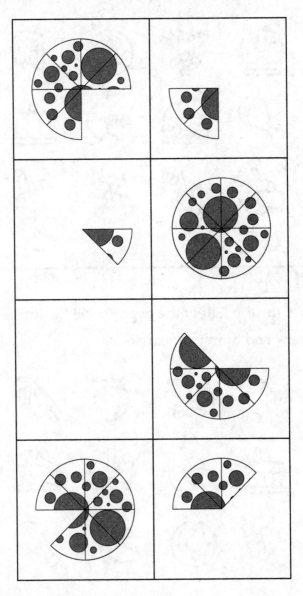

Your Logician (continued)

It proves more challenging to use information about the world to further your understanding of the rules that govern it. For instance, in puzzle **1.6 Odd One Out** (page 37), you observe evidence and from it must derive a rule that describes the organization of the shapes in four of the five arrangements. This task requires more cognitive effort than sudoku because there's more uncertainty about what constitutes "truth."

Let's Take a Breather

That was a lot of information! This chapter contains a crash course in some of the core modules you would learn if you enrolled in cognitive psychology and neuroscience classes. Well done for getting through them! But reading is one thing, remembering another. Coming back to this information after having worked through more pages of the book will help refresh your memory. In the next sections, you'll learn strategies that can help you get through these puzzles more effectively.

2.
STRENGTH TRAINING

Now that you've warmed up, let's ramp up the difficulty. Here you'll flex your cognitive muscle properly. You also will learn cognitive strategies for these tasks.

Measure Your Progress

As you move through this chapter, you may want to measure your progress. Use the Progress Notes section at the back of the book (page 186) if you wish. One great way of marking your achievements is timing yourself to see how long it takes to complete similar tasks. Do you see a difference between your first day and a week later? How about two weeks or more? Do you generate more novel ideas in the creative thinking tasks or recall more details from a previous memory task? Nothing feels more motivating than seeing how far you've come, so celebrate your success when you notice progress, even if it's just a small step.

Keep Holding On

The limited capacity of your short-term memory buffer that keeps information available for you to navigate through daily life acts as a filter that keeps the myriad stimuli around you from overwhelming you. When listening to your favorite song while waiting for the bus or train, you don't need to keep in mind the faces of the people around you, their conversations, or the smells coming from a nearby bakery.

Yet the vulnerability of short-term memory systems, which represents a major drawback, means that you often need to focus in order not to forget something that you just experienced. Attention, a universal resource needed for all complex cognitive functions, affords focus. Unfortunately, the book format doesn't lend itself to attention training well, so free up your mental resources by minimizing distractions and not switching between cognitive exercises and other tasks or actions.

The easiest strategy to use in short-term memory tasks is subvocal rehearsal. That phrase just means repeating information over and over in your head so it sticks. You probably use that one all the time. Another prominent and effective strategy for short-term memory is chunking, by which you group multiple elements into one group. Why is this effective? Bound pieces of information take up fewer resources of your short-term memory store. The simplest example is remembering the sequence 4-3-6-1 with four elements versus remembering 43 and 61 separately as two elements. Try the following puzzle using the chunking technique.

2.1 Digital Memorization

Read through each line of numbers twice, chunking any memorable groups of digits as you go. Then cover this page and rewrite the lines of digits as accurately as you can on the corresponding lines on the opposite page. Proceed line by line.

Line 1

3 1 5 7 9 1 9 4 5

Line 2

2 0 9 9 4 2 4 5 1 8

Line 2

1 7 4 5 5 9 2 4 0 9 3

Line 4

5 2 8 5 2 0 2 5 7 8 3 9

Recall

Write the digit sequences as well as you can:

Line 1

....

Line 2

....

Line 3

....

Line 4

....

Your Mind's Eye

Classic examples of visuospatial skills involve Tetris, the popular 1980s game, similar types of block puzzles, or the Rubik's Cube. In contrast to verbal short-term memory, visuospatial tasks have the added complexity of requiring recall of the identity of individual elements and the relationships among them. The chunking strategy also works for some types of visuospatial tasks. Try it with the next few puzzles and see whether this approach works for you. For some puzzles, such as **2.2 Grid Memory** (page 69), this strategy will work well. For instance, the symmetry along the diagonal of the grid in the middle provides an easy opportunity for chunking. Your brain has a preference for familiar groupings of shapes, so diagonals, Ts, rectangles, and triangles easily chunk together. Even more memorable are shapes that resemble meaningful objects.

Not all strategies work equally for a given cognitive task, as you'll see in the following puzzles. Learning how to select the most appropriate strategy works on its own as a worthwhile goal toward which to strive as you work your way through these puzzles.

2.2 Grid Memory

Study the pattern in the first grid on the left of the page, then cover it and try to reproduce it accurately in the empty grid to the right. Repeat for the second and third grids.

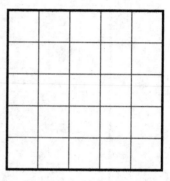

2.3 Shape Link

In each of the two puzzles below, draw a series of separate
paths that each connects a pair of identical shapes. No more
than one path can enter any square, and paths can travel only
horizontally or vertically between squares.

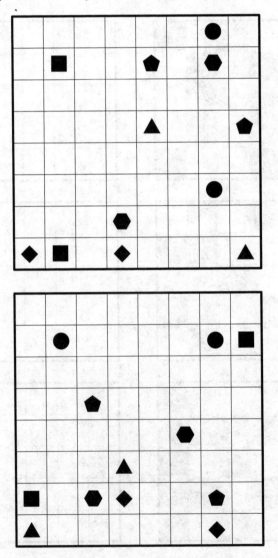

2.4 Fences

Draw horizontal and vertical lines to join all the dots in each grid into a single loop that touches every dot exactly once but doesn't cross itself. Some lines are given already.

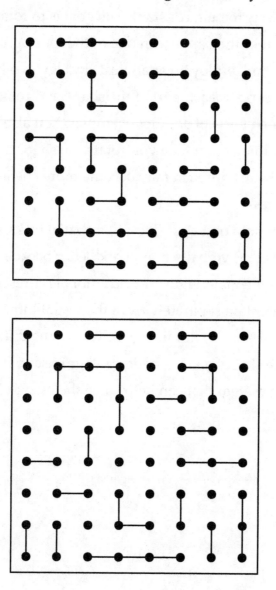

Transformative Tasks

Other classic tasks to train your visuospatial skills involve mental rotation: picturing a stimulus in your mind's eye and manipulating it to change its orientation. In **2.5 Hidden Image** (page 73), the shape and configuration of the hidden objects remain constant. The goal is to rotate them to test whether they appear in one of the four options. To do so, you can employ an analytical strategy in which you separately process each part of the shape and rotate it on its own to match parts of another exemplar. You also can use a holistic strategy in which you rotate the shape as a whole. But the holistic approach may become more challenging with larger shapes.

If you're not good at or don't like spatial tasks, describing individual steps verbally may work better because it transforms the material into an additional representation that you can maintain separately from the visual information. Using your hands to mimic the moves for the different parts of the shape (a kinesthetic strategy) uses yet another processing system that can help solve the puzzle.

2.5 Hidden Image

Which of the options, A to D, conceals the image shown
at the left? It may be rotated, but all elements of it must be
visible.

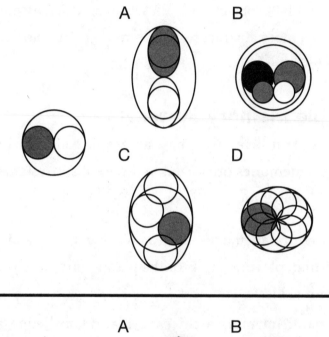

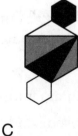

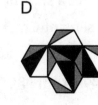

Transformative Tasks (continued)

In visuospatial construction tasks, your goal is to change the configuration of objects to create something new: a cube or some other shape, such as in **1.11 Building Blocks** (page 43) or in **2.6 Tracing Paper** (page 76). Anyone working with 3D objects uses these skills, which essentially represent a more abstract form of building with blocks or putting together a flat-pack bookshelf.

Multiple Memory Systems

Throughout our lives, we amass a sizeable collection of long-term memories organized in different subsystems of the brain. These include:

▶ **Procedural memory**—such as writing, riding a bicycle, knitting, playing tennis or the piano—supports your motor skills.

▶ **Semantic memory** archives facts and knowledge, and by virtue of partially overlapping brain networks, it collaborates closely with episodic memory, the steward of memories of past events.

▶ **Episodic memories** contain information about the context of a specific episode and the details it contains, while semantic memories mostly remain detached from the original context. While **2.9 Shakespearean Shakedown** (page 80) requires memory only for facts,

2.8 A Study in Scarlet (page 78) demands recall of context and details of the narrative.

Other neural systems and cognitive processes work hand in hand with long-term memory. For instance, unscrambling anagrams not only tests your ability to rifle through factual knowledge quickly, but it also demands that you keep subsequent candidates in mind and simultaneously use your visuospatial working memory to swap letters to test whether your guess is correct. This process taxes your short- and long-term memory abilities, and if you add the timing element to it, these types of puzzles also can improve the speed with which your brain processes information.

2.6 Tracing Paper

Which of the options, A to D, represents the view of each image shown to the left when folded in half along the dotted line? Assume the paper is transparent.

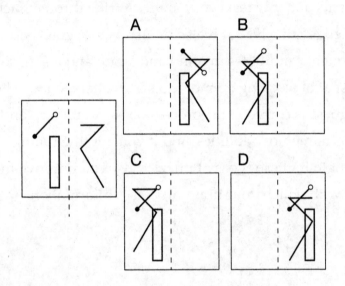

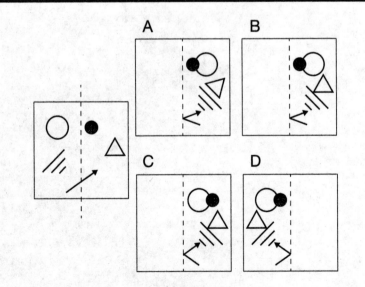

2.7 Musical Medleys

Unscramble the names of these famous musicians. The letter count for each word of the unscrambled name appears in parentheses after the anagram.

AND MOAN (7)

LIVELY SPREES (5, 7)

EVEN WORDIEST (6, 6)

NO HEN JOLT (5, 4)

SEEN HEARD (2, 7)

ARTY IT FLOWS (6, 5)

PARTY ON DOLL (5, 6)

CURT MANLY PACE (4, 9)

2.8 A Study in Scarlet

Cover the opposite page and read this page, from *A Study in Scarlet* by Arthur Conan Doyle, until you think you'll remember the phrasing used. Then continue opposite.

Holmes was certainly not a difficult man to live with. He was quiet in his ways, and his habits were regular. It was rare for him to be up after ten at night, and he had invariably breakfasted and gone out before I rose in the morning.

Sometimes he spent his day at the chemical laboratory, sometimes in the dissecting-rooms, and occasionally in long walks, which appeared to take him into the lowest portions of the City.

Nothing could exceed his energy when the working fit was upon him; but now and again a reaction would seize him, and for days on end he would lie upon the sofa in the sitting room, hardly uttering a word or moving a muscle from morning to night. On these occasions I have noticed such a dreamy, vacant expression in his eyes, that I might have suspected him of being addicted to the use of some narcotic, had not the temperance and cleanliness of his whole life forbidden such a notion.

Recall

Now cover the opposite page. In the text below, eight of the words have changed. Which eight words, and what were they before?

Holmes was certainly not a hard man to live with. He was quiet in his ways, and his habits were predictable. It was rare for him to be up after ten at night, and he had invariably eaten and gone out before I rose in the morning.

Sometimes he spent his day at the biology laboratory, sometimes in the dissecting-rooms, and occasionally in long walks, which appeared to take him into the lowest portions of the town.

Nothing could exceed his energy when the working fit was upon him; but now and again a reaction would grab him, and for days on end he would lie upon the sofa in the living room, hardly uttering a word or moving a muscle from morning to night. On these occasions I have noticed such a dreamy, empty expression in his eyes, that I might have suspected him of being addicted to the use of some narcotic, had not the temperance and cleanliness of his whole life forbidden such a notion.

2.9 Shakespearean Shakedown

Which eight plays by William Shakespeare appear abbreviated below, with only the first letter of each word in the play's title given?

A Y L I

M A A N

A M N D

T T N K

T T O T S

T T G O V

A W T E W

T M W O W

Bonded for Life

Sometimes you might wander among the halls of your archive and without any external impulse retrieve a record from your episodic memory while reminiscing. In most instances, though, you recall episodic memories prompted by a cue that activates a trace of the memory representation stored in your mental library.

You may have seen, heard, smelled, or tasted something that reminds you of a past event. If this sensation has a strong association with that experience, it can trigger a particularly vivid memory:

▶ Maybe you often ate a particular flavor of ice cream during a summer vacation;

▶ Maybe you and your best friend have a song that makes you think of good times that you shared;

▶ Maybe a famous quote from a movie reminds you of the first time you saw it ("Shaken, not stirred." "May the Force be with you!" "I'll be back!" "Florals? For spring? Groundbreaking.")

These types of cues point like lasers to a particular memory or multiple related memories in your archive, and they often simultaneously bring back a host of details associated with that memory. You even can use that memory to recall similar instances more easily, starting a chain reaction of memory dominoes. This process offers an enormous advantage over attempting to recall a memory without a strong cue, for which you have to undertake a much more exhaustive search of the contents of your archive. That's why **2.10 "C" How Your Memory Is** (page 84) is much simpler than **2.11 Fifteen Words and Minutes** (page 85): the starting letter C limits your memory search space.

The best way to form powerful memory cues involves creating associations between or among pieces of information that you want to recall. Combining this strategy with vivid mental imagery can prove even more effective.

Think of ways in which you can form associations among the images and words in **2.12 Food Swap** (page 86) or the words in the list in **2.11 Fifteen Words and Minutes** (page 85). Can you combine them into an action (throwing the suitcase out the window)? Do they share commonalities (a sticker and a ruler in a desk)? Can you connect them in a story with both words and pictures in your head?

This method works particularly well if the narrative sounds odd or funny. ("When he woke in the morning to weigh himself, he stepped on a banana placed on the scale.").

Can you associate them with an existing memory? ("On my last train journey, I spilled coffee on my seat.") Forming associations, elaborating on the to-be-remembered information, and building narratives can help you recall more information in a more holistic, long-lasting manner.

2.10 "C" How Your Memory Is

Cover everything beneath the dividing line on this page. Then study the list of words until you think you've memorized it completely. When you're ready, cover the list and reveal the instructions below the divider.

Cerulean	**Coconut**
Cabbage	**Crockery**
Creative	**Continent**
Crumble	**Cypress**

Recall

Rewrite the list you just memorized but in alphabetical order. The first two letters of each word appear below to help you.

Ca.................................

Ce.................................

Co.................................

Co.................................

Cr.................................

Cr.................................

Cr.................................

Cy.................................

2.11 Fifteen Words and Minutes

Take as long as you need to memorize the following 15 words, then continue below.

Imagination	**Elbow**
Sticker	**Stick**
Process	**Category**
Ruler	**Television**
Keyboard	**Hat**
Radiation	**Plenty**
Crossing	**Storage**
Love	

Recall

Cover the list above and try to recall all 15 words.

....

....

....

....

....

....

....

....

And then

Wait 15 minutes and turn to page 103.

2.12 Food Swap

Cover the bottom half of this page, then spend some time studying these images and the word associated with each. When you're ready, cover them and read below.

Marigold	Pencil	Banana
Shirt	Truck	Leaf
Window	Tennis	Coffee

Recall

Cover the top half of the page. Fill in the blank below each image with the same word used above.

2.13 Country Swap

Cover everything beneath the dividing line on this page. Study the list of countries until you think you've memorized it completely. When you're ready, cover the list and reveal the instructions below the divider.

Indonesia	**Brazil**
Argentina	**Malawi**
Hungary	**Jordan**
Japan	**Mexico**
Norway	**Oman**
Canada	**New Zealand**
Sierra Leone	**Portugal**

Recall

In this version of the list, some of the countries have been replaced with others, and they appear in a different order. Circle the new countries. As a bonus, which countries did they replace?

Argentina	**Malawi**
Brazil	**Montenegro**
Canada	**Norway**
Hungary	**Oman**
India	**Papua New Guinea**
Japan	**Portugal**
Jordan	**Sierra Leone**

2.14 Password Posers

Cover the opposite page, then memorize as many of the codes and passwords as you can. When you feel ready, cover this page and reveal the page opposite.

Phone unlock PIN: 038562

Online banking password: rebmemeR1001

WiFi password: 10int29er38net47pass56

Laptop login code: l3tm31n

TV streaming PIN: m4o5v6i7e

Work email password: topsecret1995

Utility bills PIN: 000884

Home computer password: Home72Screen

Recall

The same passwords appear below in the same order, but each has changed. Can you spot the change to each line and say what the original code or password was?

Phone unlock PIN: 039562

Online banking password: RebmemeR1001

WiFi password: 10int29ern38et47pass56

Laptop login code: l3tM31n

TV streaming PIN: m4o5v6i7e8

Work email password: topsecret1999

Utility bills PIN: 008884

Home computer password: Homes72Screen

The Critical Thinker

Logic and reasoning allow you to arrive at correct conclusions about the world. Finding these rules and patterns in the information around you helps you make predictions and solve complex problems. Think of the brain as a superb prediction machine that constantly accumulates new data to check whether its knowledge about the world is up to date and that uses these predictions to guide your behavior. Making a prediction allows you to respond more quickly to events in your environment and to plan accordingly. For instance, if you know that the next train will leave in 10 minutes, but you need 12 minutes to walk to the station, you can conclude that you won't make it in time by walking. But maybe you can jog or jump on a bicycle instead.

2.15 Sudoku 9×9

Complete this sudoku puzzle by placing a digit from 1 to 9 into each empty square so that no digit repeats in any row, column, or bold-lined 3×3 box.

4	1			6			9	5
9		5				6		4
	3						2	
			8		9			
8								3
			6		5			
	2						1	
1		4				8		2
3	8			5			4	9

2.16 Number Pyramid

Write a number in each empty block so that every block (above the bottom level) equals the sum of the two blocks directly beneath it.

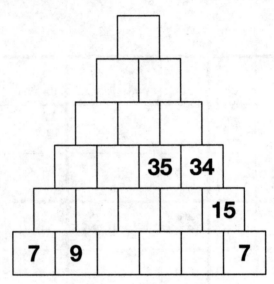

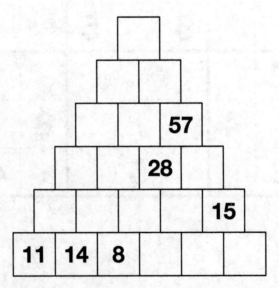

The Critical Thinker (continued)

In contrast to sudoku, the following visuospatial abstract reasoning puzzles don't give you a rule. You have to crack the code on your own. Tasks like these often feature in intelligence (IQ) tests.

There's more than just one type of intelligence (linguistic or social intelligence for instance), so tests of reasoning that involve these types of visuospatial material have the advantage that they don't rely on language and are influenced less by cultural differences among people around the world. They also tend to indicate performance in the fields of science, technology, engineering, and mathematics. However, people who excel at these types of logical tests aren't necessarily the same ones who stand out when reasoning tasks involve language.

The simplest way to approach these exercises is to write down the steps you're using to try to solve them. Consider **2.17 Crack the Code** (page 95). Write down commonalities you observe among images, note all options that may describe true relationships among shapes and letters, then test each statement and eliminate options that don't work.

Also look for evidence that could disprove your idea about the rule. Once people have a suspicion, most search only for evidence in favor of but not against the hypothesis, a common fallacy called confirmation bias that permeates much reasoning in everyday life.

2.17 Crack the Code

Crack the code used to describe each image and pick which option, 1 to 4, should replace the question mark.

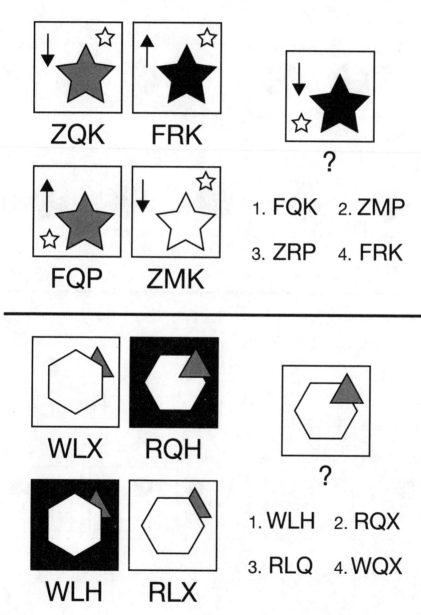

ZQK   FRK

FQP   ZMK

?

1. FQK   2. ZMP

3. ZRP   4. FRK

WLX   RQH

WLH   RLX

?

1. WLH   2. RQX

3. RLQ   4. WQX

2.18 Complete the Sequence

Which of the options, A to E, should go in the empty box on each top row to create a logical sequence?

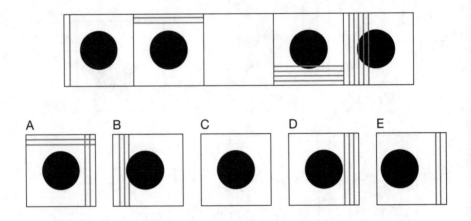

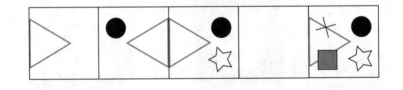

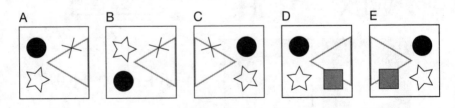

2.19 Complete the Square

Which of the four options, A to D, should go into the empty square in each grid to complete the pattern?

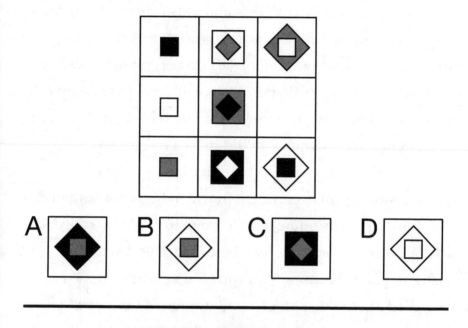

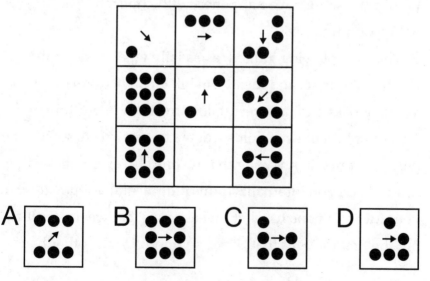

Your Inner Child to the Rescue

The mind of a child has truly amazing creative potential. For children, mundane objects can become tools entirely removed from their original purpose. They conjure new worlds, give voices to puppets and plush animals, and dress up as warriors to save the world. Who cares if they run around squealing, wearing metal strainers on their heads to protect from dragon attacks? But we all have to grow up at some point and use that wooden spoon for stirring food in a pan rather than waving it in the air as a magic wand.

Creativity researcher Robert McKim at Stanford University ran an experiment in which he asked students to draw a person sitting next to them in class. He called "stop" after 30 seconds, leading to much embarrassed laughter and shouts of "I'm sorry!" The adults in the room worried about what others would think of their creation. Would the same have happened with children? The answer is a resounding no.

That fear of being judged, especially when generating unusual thoughts and ideas, can kill creativity. We don't take as many risks and, as a result, lose freedom in our thinking. This impairment even holds true when you create something only for yourself, knowing that no one else ever will see it. Most likely, you internalized this judgmental attitude toward your ideas. On one hand, it makes sense that we don't blurt out the first thought that comes to mind. On the other hand, if we censor ourselves too much, we stop offering novel ideas. It may seem too risky. Design firms in particular have identified this as a major problem, and many now foster a more relaxed, friendly, less judgmental environment. After all, if we feel less judged, we may feel less anxious or hesitant to share a design or new idea with our peers—even if it seems wacky.

A good approach to reduce the influence of your inner critic is to give yourself a time limit to generate as many solutions to a problem as possible. It will help you suppress a tendency to second-guess yourself because your goal is quantity quickly. A great example of a creativity task that helps you loosen up and suppress that inner critic is **2.21 Eighteen Circles** (page 101) in which you have three minutes to transform eighteen empty circles into objects.

Another classic exercise is to come up with as many unusual uses for a common object. You know what a paper clip normally does, but you can use it as a lock pick, to remove dirt from under your fingernails, to open SIM cards in phones, and on and on. If your inner critic tends to be particularly strong, complete **2.20 Object-ive Thinking** below and set yourself a time limit.

2.20 Object-ive Thinking

How many unusual uses does the object listed below have? Write down as many as you can think of and avoid including anything that it "normally" does.

desk lamp

....

....

....

....

....

....

....

....

....

....

2.21 Eighteen Circles

Using your imagination, draw as many varied pictures as you can that each use one of the circles below.

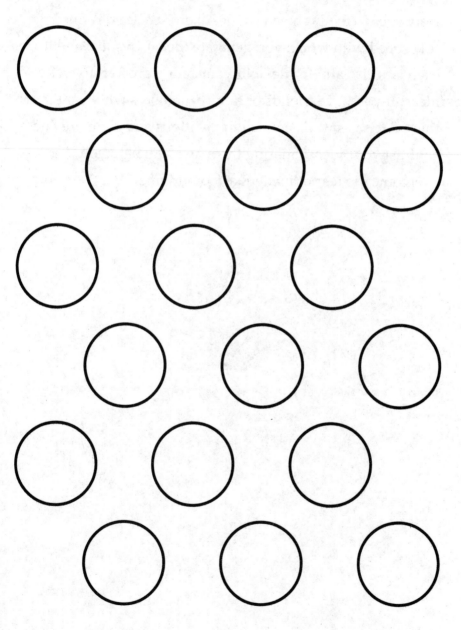

Your Inner Child to the Rescue (continued)

Reflect on your solutions to puzzles 2.20 and 2.21. Do they share a common theme, or are they variations of the same idea, such as a soccer ball, basketball, and tennis ball as responses to the Eighteen Circles exercise? Besides fluency (the speed with which you generate ideas), in subsequent exercises also aim for flexibility, meaning greater diversity of ideas. If you have friends or family members who want to try this exercise as well, share your creations and compare and contrast your ideas. Sharing them also will help you overcome the fear of inadequacy or judgment.

Recall (continued from page 85)

If you haven't done the exercise on page 85, complete
that first. When 15 minutes have passed, how many of the
15 words can you still remember? Write as many as you
can on the lines below.

....

....

....

....

....

....

....

....

....

....

....

....

....

2.22 Cube Counting

How many cubes does each of the following images have?
Each began as a 4×4×4 block before some cubes were
removed. None of the cubes is "floating" in midair.

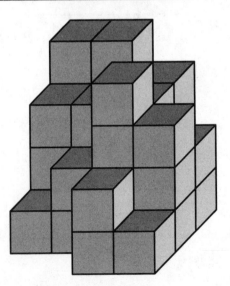

2.23 What's Missing?

The eight boxes below contain eight steps in a logical
sequence jumbled out of order. One of the boxes is empty,
however. Draw the correct picture in it.

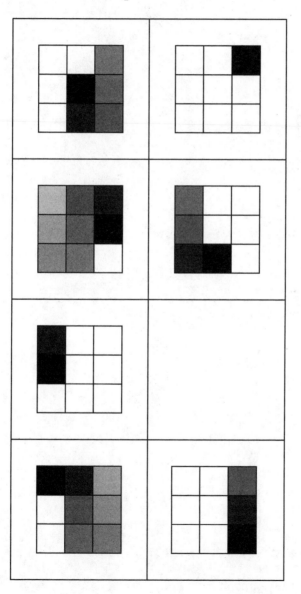

3.

CARDIO

Are you ready to take on the most demanding tasks in our cardio puzzle challenge? Cardio literally means heart rather than brain, but it's still a useful term to get you to picture a demanding, high-intensity exercise meant to help you make progress.

Before you attempt the puzzles in this chapter, make sure to complete some or all of the warm-up exercises and some or all of the strength-training puzzles. This chapter aims to challenge you even more, applying the strategies that you already know and teaching you new ones. The puzzles are intended to be difficult but hopefully will come easier with time and practice.

Dealing with Adversity

When you feel overwhelmed by any of these exercises, take your time to solve the puzzle, mull it over, maybe come back to it after a break. Sometimes entering a new environment can help with generating new ideas. Splitting bigger tasks into subcomponents can help isolate particular aspects of a problem by working through them step by step. Especially for reasoning tasks, rephrasing the problems in your own words, writing them down yourself, and organizing them into a structure that feels intuitive to you also can help with particularly tricky exercises.

Let's jump in!

Best Buddies

Short- and long-term memory make good pals. When we recall an old memory, its contents come "online" in a consciously accessible state by short-term memory. You can use this connection to your advantage. If you are given a list of digits, such as the six numbers in the phone PIN in **3.1 Password Posers** (page 110), you can try to recall them by rehearsing them in your head and applying the chunking technique, but you also can draw on your long-term memory to create a meaningful connection between the numbers and your prior knowledge. Born in 1962? Live in number 85 on your street? Now you can draw on the chunking method and meaningful information that you won't forget easily. This strategy also will make it more likely for you to remember the information in the long run. The same goes when you can find patterns that govern the information you try to recall. (1-3-5-7 is much easier to remember than 9-2-6-0.) Can you find any in the WiFi password (page 89)? What happens if you come back to those tomorrow or next week?

3.1 Password Posers

Return to the memory exercise on page 88 and memorize all the codes and passwords. When you think you've done so, return here and fill in the blanks below.

Phone unlock PIN:

....

Online banking password:

....

WiFi password:

....

Laptop login code:

....

TV streaming PIN:

....

Work email password:

....

Utility bills PIN:

....

Home computer password:

....

3.2 Olympic Scramble

Unscramble the names of these Olympic sports, which may feature at either the Summer or Winter Games. Each sport's name consists of a single word, so ignore any spaces in the anagrams.

GLUE

LION BATH

MIND TO BAN

CHEAT LIST

KEEN SLOT

I WRONG

QUIET EARNS

BOO WINS GRAND

BRAKE SAINT GOD

The Art of Storytelling

As you now know, different mnemonic strategies lend themselves to different types of material. To recall details and facts from text, you can use the PQRST strategy. It stands for preview, question, read, state, and test. This technique originally helped aid students' reading comprehension, but it also can help you to recall information from text at a later time. In a rapid preview of the text, quickly identify the overarching theme that serves as a memory scaffold, drawing on general background knowledge already solidly anchored in your mental library. Formulate questions about the information in the text that more actively engage you versus reading in a more passive voice. Questioning also sharpens your focus on specific elements of the text. Then read the text more carefully and state your answers to the questions that you formulated. Finally, test yourself on the amount of recalled information. As you will see, posing questions = richer storytelling.

Making acronyms of more complex terms serves as a helpful memory strategy in itself, but what happens when the acronym is too long and you can't remember even your memory aid? Creating something more memorable, such as a sentence with semantic meaning, can become an even more powerful tool. You may forget each step for this strategy if you have only the letters PQRST to go on, but if you try to remember it by remembering the "posing questions = richer storytelling" method, you more likely can recall each step. If you can find one, a rhyming sentence works even better—no wonder you probably recall the lyrics to countless songs!

For the following memory puzzles, try out these new strategies. Use what you learned in Chapter 2 and draw on strategies that strengthen associations, paint vivid mental images and stories, and organize material into a format that suits you best to commit it to long-term memory. For **3.24 Face Off** (page 144), try to form associations among a name and the specific features and idiosyncrasies of the person: Dave has spiky hair like a crown. Maybe you could use King David as a memory cue.

3.3 Recounting Dracula

Cover the text on the opposite page and read the following text, taken from *Dracula* by Bram Stoker, one or two times through. Then continue opposite.

"3 May. Bistritz.—Left Munich at 8:35 PM, on 1st May, arriving at Vienna early next morning; should have arrived at 6:46, but train was an hour late. Buda-Pesth seems a wonderful place, from the glimpse which I got of it from the train and the little I could walk through the streets. I feared to go very far from the station, as we had arrived late and would start as near the correct time as possible. The impression I had was that we were leaving the West and entering the East; the most western of splendid bridges over the Danube, which is here of noble width and depth, took us among the traditions of Turkish rule.

We left in pretty good time, and came after nightfall to Klausenburgh. Here I stopped for the night at the Hotel Royale. I had for dinner, or rather supper, a chicken done up some way with red pepper, which was very good but thirsty. (Memorandum: get recipe for Mina). I asked the waiter, and he said it was called "paprika hendl," and that, as it was a national dish, I should be able to get it anywhere along the Carpathians. I found my smattering of German very useful here; indeed, I don't know how I should be able to get on without it."

Recall

Cover the opposite page. Answer the following questions about the extract from *Dracula* that you just read.

1. On what date was the diary entry written?

2. At what time did the writer say they left Munich?

3. How late was the train arriving into Vienna?

4. Which river does the narrator describe as having "splendid bridges"?

5. What is the name of the hotel where the writer stayed?

6. For whom did the narrator intend to obtain a recipe?

7. Which mountain range does the writer mention, in reference to the dish he ate?

8. Of which language does the writer have "a smattering"?

3.4 Winning Words

Study this partial list of Oscar winners for best picture, listed in reverse chronological order, until you've memorized them. When ready, cover the list and proceed below.

Nomadland	**Titanic**
Parasite	**Braveheart**
Moonlight	**Unforgiven**
Spotlight	**Platoon**
Argo	**Amadeus**
Crash	**Gandhi**
Chicago	**Rocky**
Gladiator	**Patton**

Recall

Can you recall all of the movies?

....

....

....

....

....

....

....

Master Manipulator

You've learned strategies for visuospatial short-term memory and mental rotation tasks. You can use verbalization to transform visual information, rotate parts of an object at a time or choose a holistic approach, chunk parts of the image to reduce memory load, or combine these strategies for even better results. Here, you have the opportunity to build on these skills further. You might want to observe your use of strategies as you tackle these tasks. What's your preferred strategy? Does it depend on the type of task? Use the space below to note your strategies.

....

....

....

....

....

....

....

....

....

....

3.5 Odd One Out

Which of the images, A to E, is the odd one out from each set and why?

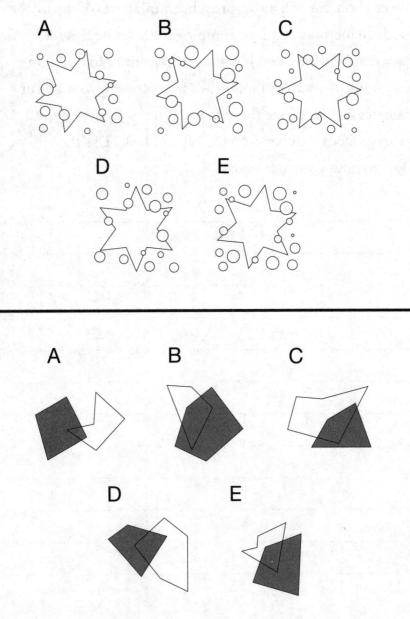

3.6 Squaring Up

How many total squares of all sizes (1×1, 2×2, and so on) can you count in this grid?

What about with this 4×4 grid? How many squares of all sizes does it contain?

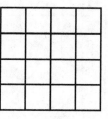

How about with this 5×5 grid? How many squares of all sizes do you count?

Can you work out a general method of calculating the number of squares in a square grid of any size, x by x?

3.7 Building Blocks

In the two puzzles below, which set of blocks, A to D, can you rearrange to form the assembly shown? All blocks must be used exactly once each.

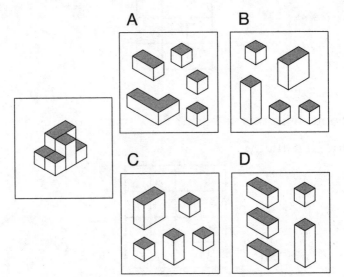

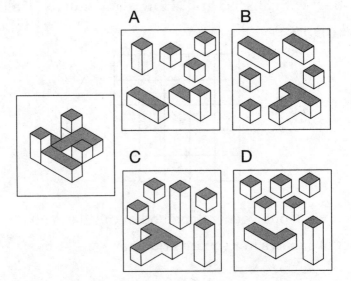

3.8 Cube Counting

How many cubes does each of the following images have?
Each began as a 4×4×4 block before some cubes were
removed. None of the cubes is floating in midair.

3.9 Grid Memory

Study the pattern in the first grid on the left of the page, then cover it and try to reproduce it accurately in the empty grid to the right. Repeat for the second grid.

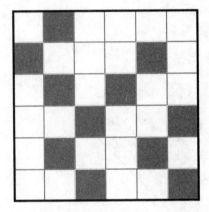 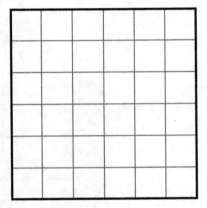

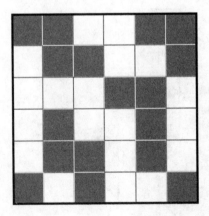

3.10 Hidden Image

Which of the options, A to D, conceals the image shown at left? It may be rotated, but all elements of it must be visible.

A

B

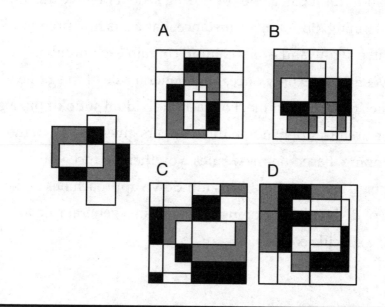

A

B

C

D

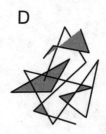

A

B

C

D

The Art of Deduction

Deduction allows you to draw specific conclusions from general information about the world, which here we'll call premises. Many examples of numerical reasoning and logic in standard puzzle games or during school involve this type of reasoning. Sudoku, for instance, has as its first premise that every row and every column contain each number between 1 and 9 only once. That general rule of the game applies to each example. For each individual sudoku puzzle, other premises depend on the numbers given to you in the beginning. Based on these rules, you then deduce which numbers belong where. This top-down approach lies at the core of deductive reasoning: going from a general rule to derive specific conclusions.

3.11 Blackout Sudoku

Place a digit from 1 to 9 into every empty white square
so that no digit repeats in any row, column, or bold-lined
3×3 box. Shaded squares must remain empty. Be careful,
however. They don't always represent the same digit in each
row, column, or 3×3 box.

6	1		7	9		▓	8	4
▓		7			4			3
			▓	5	3		7	
	5	6		4	▓	9		8
2		▓	5		1	7		6
7		3		8		1	5	▓
	▓		9	2	8			
9			4			5	▓	2
8	7			▓	5		9	1

3.12 Number Pyramid

Write a number in each empty block so that every block (above the bottom level) equals the sum of the two blocks directly beneath it.

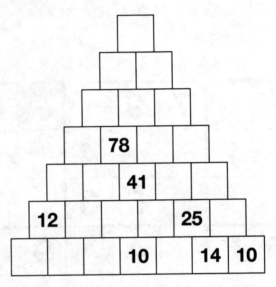

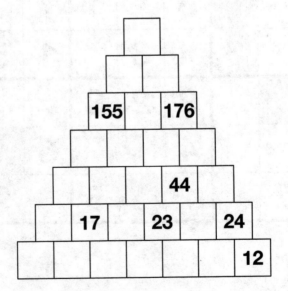

3.13 Jigdoku

Complete this jigdoku puzzle by placing a letter from A to G into each empty square so that no letter repeats in any row, column, or bold-lined jigsaw shape.

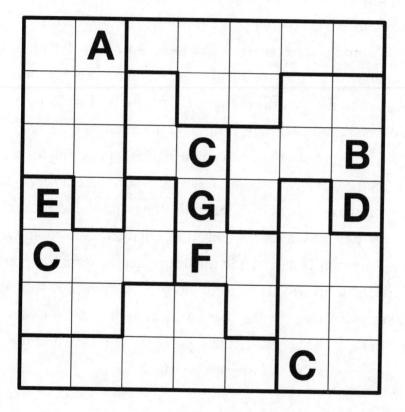

The Art of Deduction (continued)

Can you do the same for verbal reasoning? Let's look at an example.

▶ Premise 1: Londoners live in England.

▶ Premise 2: England is part of Britain.

Assuming that both of these statements are true, we can say with absolute certainty that Londoners live in Britain.

Within the framework of this logical problem, let's say someone told you that she met some English guy in a pub. She concludes that the man must have been a Londoner. Unless she asked him to verify where specifically he lives, you can point out that she can't be sure that her conclusion holds true. You can add smugly that her statement serves as a typical example of overgeneralization without verification.

Mathematicians and scientists use deductive reasoning all the time, and you used it in the train example from Chapter 2. That the train will arrive in 10 minutes is premise 1. That it takes you no fewer than 12 minutes on foot to the station is premise 2. The conclusion that you can't get there on time if you go on foot therefore *must* be true.

Elementary

Real life is often messy, and you may not know whether a general premise is definitely correct. In that case, inductive reasoning may help you determine whether specific observations can help you draw a general conclusion:

▶ You see a dog in the park, and it lets you pet it;

▶ You see a dog sitting next to an infant without harming the child;

▶ You encounter dogs in many other positive situations, and you conclude that dogs are friendly, nice to be around, and won't hurt you.

That conclusion doesn't have to be true based on the evidence you've accumulated, rather it *may* be true. If you then hear about a dog biting a postman, it doesn't mean that your conclusion about dogs is entirely false. It means that *most* but not all dogs are friendly.

Inductive reasoning therefore doesn't provide certainty, only likely conclusions. It follows a bottom-up approach going from specific examples to general rules—the opposite of what you do in deductive reasoning. The more observations you make of dogs, the more confident you can be in your hypothesis that dogs tend to be friendly toward humans.

You employ inductive reasoning constantly, simply by using observations from the past to predict the future. This strategy proves effective because the rules that led to past events often still remain valid in the future.

Inductive reasoning has its pitfalls, though. Sometimes you can't predict the future from the past. Also, your specific experience of the past defines your preconceptions that will affect your conclusions and predictions. Biases are normal. We all are human after all and working with a limited set of knowledge and experience.

But what should you do to confront your biases? Be like Sherlock Holmes, who famously said: "When you have eliminated the impossible, whatever remains, however improbable, must be the truth." Simply put, look at all the evidence before jumping to conclusions and determine whether a problem may have multiple possible explanations or solutions. The correct solution may not always be the most obvious.

If possible, seek other means of gathering more information and, step by step, eliminate options incompatible with all the data that you've collected. In the end, choose the option most likely to hold true.

Devising puzzles for this type of reasoning can prove challenging, so the best way to get into this logical mindset is to apply it to an observation in real life for which an explanation isn't obvious; or use it for a complex problem in school, work, or elsewhere in life.

For now, continue with the following puzzles that employ more abstract visuospatial reasoning tasks. They combine aspects of inductive and deductive reasoning as you follow patterns and infer rules.

3.14 What's Missing?

The boxes below contain eight steps in a logical sequence jumbled out of order. One of the boxes is empty, however. Draw the correct picture in it.

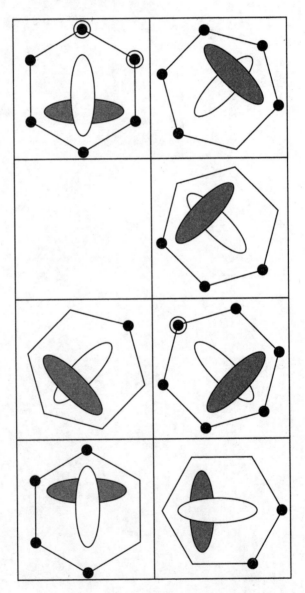

3.15 Complete the Sequence

Which of the options, A to E, should go in the empty box on each top row to create a logical sequence?

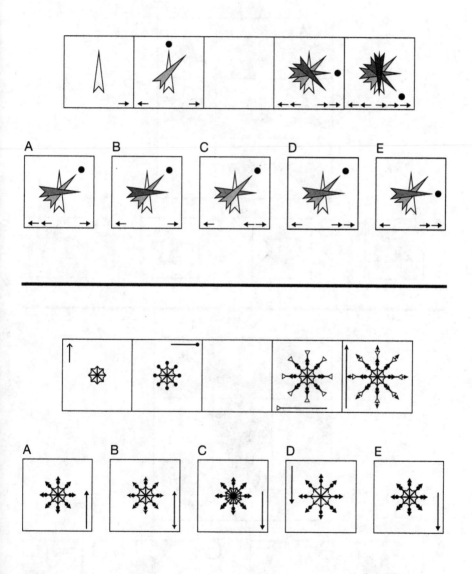

3.16 Complete the Square

Which of the four options, A to D, should go in the empty square in each grid to complete the pattern?

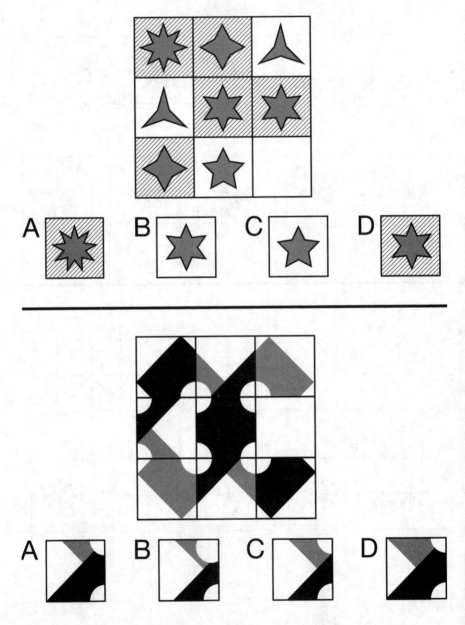

Beyond the Pages

For many people, everyday life, be it leisure or work, doesn't provide many opportunities for creative thinking. That's a shame because creativity, coming up with something completely new, can feel incredibly rewarding and help prevent your brain from falling into a rut. Even in later years at school, teaching and learning mostly focus on learning facts, or logic and reasoning, with answers to tests often being either right or wrong. Let's break that mold, and for the next three challenges, gather a notepad and pen and let's take a break from these pages for a while.

POINTS

3.17 Writing Practice

Recall a recent memory that involved another person. Rewrite that memory from the other person's perspective, adding thoughts that the person might have had in the moment.

▶ Why did the person act in that way?

▶ What were the person's goals?

▶ What did the person think about you in that moment and why?

3.18 Time Traveler

Imagine how time travelers from the Middle Ages or the Roman Empire would describe our technologies and way of life.

▶ What would surprise them?

▶ What would they find ridiculous?

▶ What in our world goes against their morals?

▶ How would they explain our world to a person from their time who has seen nothing from our future?

3.19 Transport Designer

Experiment with using your visual creativity by drawing a design for a new means of transportation. It can involve any method of movement that you can imagine.

Beyond the Pages (continued)

It may seem nonsensical to do exercises such as **3.18 Time Traveler** (page 136). What good do they do? Quite a bit actually—

▶ Novel experiences challenge your brain and create new connections.

▶ You become more accustomed to generating lots of new ideas.

▶ You actively engage your cognitive processes to *do* something rather than just passively receiving information.

▶ You learn to judge yourself less.

▶ Hopefully, you also have fun.

Getting in the habit of not following habits can prove quite challenging and may sound contradictory. It simply means becoming more comfortable with trying something new and challenging your preconceptions. A brain given varied experiences naturally has more information from which it can generate novel ideas and solve complex problems.

Finally, it helps to remember that the best path for tackling complex problems often entails a combination of divergent thinking, which uses creativity to generate novel ideas, and convergent thinking, which uses logical reasoning to evaluate these ideas critically. Use your logic, challenge your preconceptions, and don't leave out unusual ideas.

Hopefully, after you engage in this type of thinking more frequently within these pages, you give yourself more freedom to approach situations in real life with this type of mindset in the future.

3.20 About the House

Study the order of this list of rooms in a house. When you've memorized the list, turn the page and follow the instructions. You will be asked to recall only the order in which the rooms appeared, not the rooms themselves.

1. **Kitchen**
2. **Study**
3. **Lounge**
4. **Bathroom**
5. **Living Room**
6. **Basement**
7. **Utility Room**
8. **Garage**
9. **Bedroom**
10. **Library**
11. **Nursery**
12. **Closet**
13. **Porch**
14. **Hallway**
15. **Attic**
16. **Pantry**
17. **Mudroom**
18. **Workshop**

Recall (from previous page)

The same list of rooms now appears in alphabetical order.
Write the number next to each room below to show its
original position in the list on the previous page.

.... **Attic**
.... **Basement**
.... **Bathroom**
.... **Bedroom**
.... **Closet**
.... **Garage**
.... **Hallway**
.... **Kitchen**
.... **Library**
.... **Living Room**
.... **Lounge**
.... **Mudroom**
.... **Nursery**
.... **Pantry**
.... **Porch**
.... **Study**
.... **Utility Room**
.... **Workshop**

3.21 Shape Link

Draw a series of separate paths, each connecting a pair of identical shapes. No more than one path can enter any square, and paths can travel only horizontally or vertically between squares.

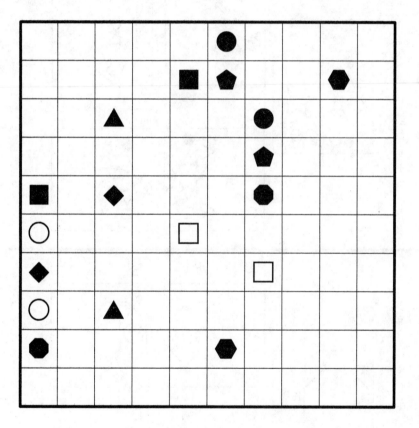

3.22 Tracing Paper

Which of the options, A to D, represents the view of the image shown to the left when folded in half along the dotted line? Assume the paper is transparent.

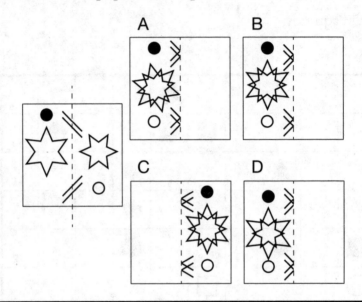

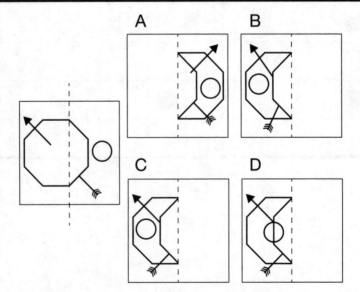

3.23 Careful Counting

How many rectangles and squares of any size appear in the
following picture? It contains more than you might think,
and don't forget to include the outside shape!

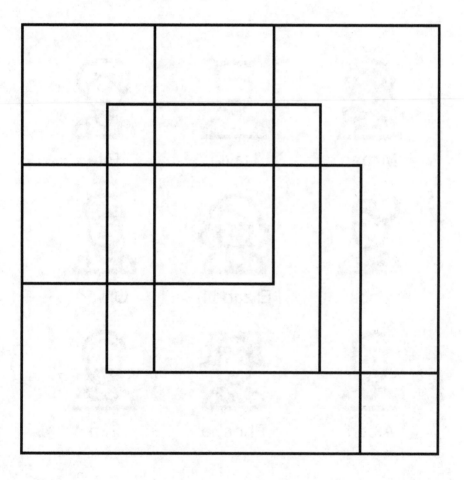

3.24 Face Off

Cover the opposite page, then spend two minutes studying these names and faces. When you've memorized which name goes with which face, cover this page and read the instructions opposite.

 Megan

 David

 Rita

 Jack

 Elizabeth

 Oliver

 Albert

 Phoebe

 Tim

Recall

All but three of the faces from the opposite page appear again here. First fill in the blanks beneath the faces with the correct names, then use the spaces at the bottom to write in the names of the three missing faces.

_____   _____   _____

_____   _____   _____

_____   _____   _____

4.
COOL DOWN

Any intense physical exercise should end with a restorative stretch and a cool-down. For your brain exercises, finishing with some simpler puzzles will keep you from feeling too discouraged if the more challenging exercises felt frustrating at times or if you found it difficult to progress. These puzzles will remind you of your solid, basic cognitive skill set.

The cool-down also will provide you with a chance to reflect on your experiences during tasks you found most challenging: What went well? What seemed particularly difficult? Taking notes on your accomplishments and your new goals can help structure your next puzzle session and keep you motivated. It also will help you identify the types of strategies that you may want to practice more. Use the **Progress Notes** (page 186) if you wish.

You have read a great deal about various types of puzzles. Rather than teaching you yet more strategies or touting more health advice, this chapter includes stories of some of the fascinating people who inadvertently led neuroscientists to uncover some of the mysteries of the brain.

Learning from Patients

We often learn better when presented with stories rather than dry facts. The stories of these patients are tragic yet intriguing, and because our brains tend to remember information with emotional content, the stories also serve as an effective vehicle for knowledge about the organization of the human brain. Until the advent of neuroimaging methods that now allow scientists to study the brains of healthy, conscious humans while they perform tasks in a brain scanner, researchers had only one way to map the functions of specific brain regions in humans: observing the behavior of patients who suffered from medical conditions or accidents that damaged parts of their brains. Despite the challenges and suffering that these and many other patients had to endure because of their injuries, their contributions to cognitive neuroscience remain an important legacy.

Brain regions at the back of your head are first to receive visual information from the eyes. From there, different regions process information about an object's identity, while others register spatial information about that object's position in the environment, and yet others combine this information at later stages in the visual processing hierarchy. This organization of visual information processing can lead to seemingly odd patterns of behavior when certain regions of the brain sustain injury. For instance, patient D.F., with damage to parts of the processing stream for object recognition, could catch a ball but couldn't name or copy a picture of an apple.

Blindsighted

Even more fascinating is what researchers refer to as blindsight. Some patients with damage to early visual brain areas become unconscious of objects in their visual field, leading to a form of blindness in which their eyes see but their brains don't. This condition goes by the medical name agnosopsia, which means not knowing what one sees. If you showed an apple to someone with this condition and asked what object you were holding, the person wouldn't know that you were holding anything at all, let alone be capable of naming the object. Yet in many cases, these patients still retain the ability to move their eyes to look at or even point to that object. These surprising medical cases show how information outside our awareness still can guide our actions, raising interesting questions about the nature of human consciousness that neuroscientists have yet to answer.

4.1 Top-Down Problem

Which of the options, A to D, represents the view of each 3D object when seen from the direction of the arrow?

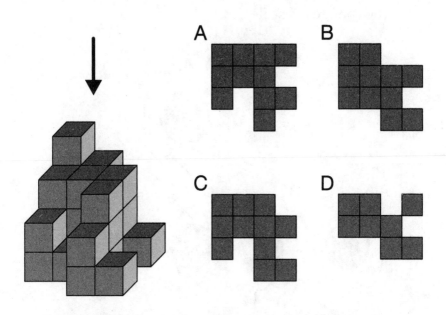

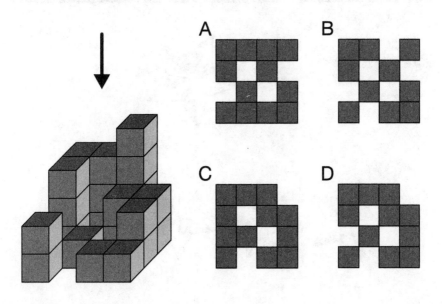

4.2 Reflect on This

Imagine reflecting each of these two images across the dotted lines shown. Which lower image, A to D, results in each case? Ignore the changes in scale.

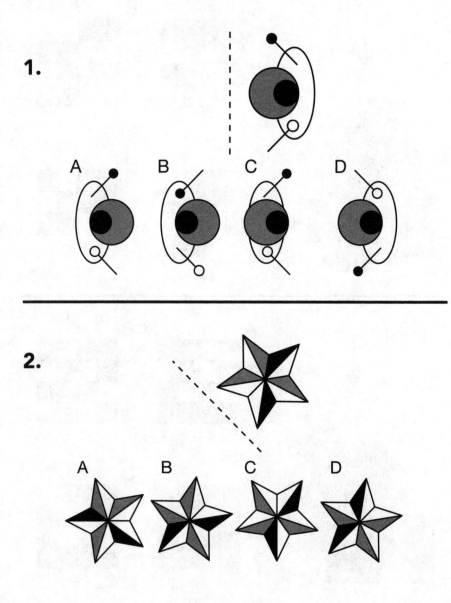

1.

A   B   C   D

2.

A   B   C   D

4.3 Shape Link

Draw a series of separate paths, each connecting a pair
of identical shapes. No more than one path can enter any
square, and paths can travel only horizontally or vertically
between squares.

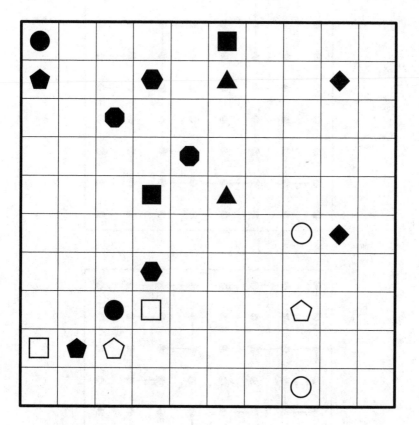

4.4 Fences

Draw horizontal and vertical lines to join all the dots in each grid into a single loop that connects every dot exactly once but doesn't cross itself.

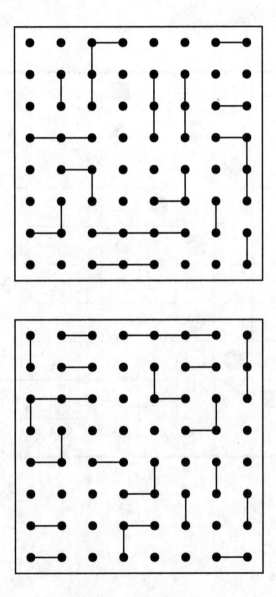

4.5 Fold and Punch

Imagine folding and then punching paper as shown in each of the two puzzles. Unfold, and which image, A to D, results?

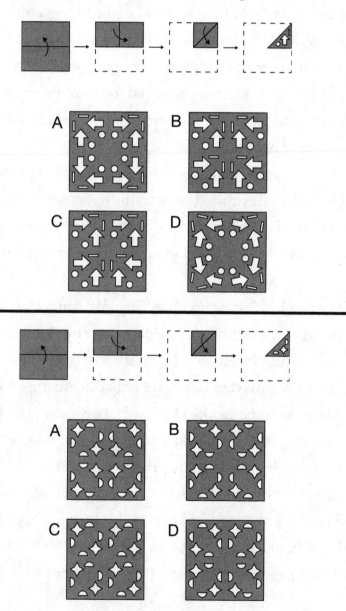

Caught in the Present

The most famous patient with a brain lesion was Henry
Molaison (known scientifically until his death as H.M.).

The treatment he received for medication-resistant
epilepsy consisted of the removal of the hippocampus, the
brain region doctors later identified as necessary to form
long-term memories for personally experienced events and
new knowledge. H.M. represented the most prominent case
of anterograde amnesia: meaning that he lost the ability
to form new memories and lost recent memories from his
life prior to surgery, yet his older memories, language,
and knowledge acquired prior to the operation remained.
His ability to learn new facts almost entirely disappeared,
but he could acquire novel motor skills and maintained
above average intelligence.

Another tragic case involves Clive Wearing, a professional
musician whose brain sustained damage from a severe
herpes simplex infection causing lesions in the same
brain area removed in H.M. Not only did Wearing have
anterograde amnesia like H.M., with new memories not
formed, but he also had retrograde amnesia, unable to recall
most memories from his life prior to the infection.

Called "30-Second Clive," Wearing perpetually had the
feeling of just waking from a coma, his life largely constrained
to the contents of his short-term memory, which never made
it into his long-term memory. The connections among his

short-term buffer and his archives for facts and personally experienced events essentially had severed. Though Wearing had forgotten the names of his children, he remembered his love for his wife and joyously greeted her every time she entered the room, even if she had been gone only briefly. He retained the ability to learn new motor skills and remained capable of playing complex musical pieces, even though he couldn't recall their titles or composers. These remarkable cases of memory damage and maintenance demonstrate a divide between learning factual information and utilizing or acquiring motor skills, as well as between the recall of old memories and the formation of novel ones.

4.6 A Gem of a Challenge

Cover everything below the dividing line on this page. Then spend a few minutes memorizing this list of precious stones. When you're ready, cover the list and reveal the instructions below.

Ruby	Moonstone
Beryl	Pearl
Sapphire	Opal
Peridot	Emerald
Onyx	Topaz
Jet	Coral
Garnet	Diamond

Recall

Write out the list of gemstones again. To help you, the final letter of each stone appears below, but the stones appear in reverse order from above.

....................d	....................t
....................l	....................t
....................z	x
....................d	....................t
....................l	....................e
....................l	l
....................e	....................y

4.7 Grid Memory

Study the pattern in the first grid on the left of the page, then cover it and try reproduce it accurately in the empty grid to the right. Repeat for the second and third grids.

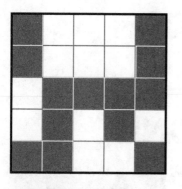
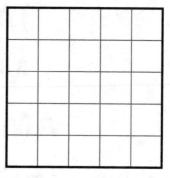

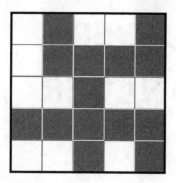

4.8 Fruity Finding

How quickly can you unscramble the names of these fruits?
Each fruit's name is a single word, so ignore any spaces or
punctuation in the anagrams.

TADE

MILE

AMONG

TROPICA

PLAIN PEEP

MAD TRAIN

AREN'T NICE

REBEL DRYER

POET MANAGER

4.9 Musical Memory

Cover everything below the dividing line on this page.
Then spend a few minutes memorizing this list of musical
instruments. When you're ready, cover the list and reveal the
instructions below.

Guitar	**Oboe**
Sitar	**Tuba**
Harmonica	**Violin**
Saxophone	**Harp**
Timpani	**Bugle**
Glockenspiel	**Double bass**
Mandolin	**Piano**

Recall

Write out the list of instruments again. To help you, the first
letter of each instrument appears below, although the first
letters now run in alphabetical order.

B..............................	**O**..............................
D..............................	**P**..............................
G..............................	**S**..............................
G..............................	**S**..............................
H..............................	**T**..............................
H..............................	**T**..............................
M..............................	**V**..............................

4.10 Poor Little Women

Cover the text on the opposite page. Now read the following text, taken from *Little Women* by Louisa May Alcott, one or two times. Then continue opposite.

"Christmas won't be Christmas without any presents," grumbled Jo, lying on the rug.

"It's so dreadful to be poor!" sighed Meg, looking down at her old dress.

"I don't think it's fair for some girls to have plenty of pretty things, and other girls nothing at all," added little Amy, with an injured sniff.

"We've got Father and Mother, and each other," said Beth contentedly from her corner.

The four young faces on which the firelight shone brightened at the cheerful words, but darkened again as Jo said sadly, "We haven't got Father, and shall not have him for a long time." She didn't say "perhaps never," but each silently added it, thinking of Father far away, where the fighting was.

Recall

Now cover the opposite page. The text below reads almost identical to the original—but not quite. Which ten words have changed?

"Christmas won't be Christmas without any gifts," grumbled Jo, lying on the carpet.

"It's so awful to be poor!" sighed Meg, looking down at her old skirt.

"I don't think it's fair for some girls to have plenty of lovely things, and other girls nothing at all," added little Amy, with an unhappy sniff.

"We've got Father and Mother, and each other," said Beth reassuringly from her corner.

The four youthful faces on which the firelight shone brightened at the cheerful words, but fell again as Jo said sadly, "We haven't got Father, and shall not have him for a long time." She didn't say "perhaps never," but each silently added it, thinking of Father far away, where the war was.

4.11 Password Posers

Cover everything below the dividing line, then spend up to 1 minute memorizing these six codes and passwords. When the time is up, reveal the text beneath.

Bank card PIN:	**1290**
Email password:	**Mail44**
Computer login:	**H4RDdr1v3**
Internet access:	**hom3OnLiNe**
Voicemail PIN:	**101012**
Family cloud:	**BakerPhotos2022**

Recall

Cover the top of the page, then fill in the blanks below with the codes and passwords, which appear in a different order than above.

Voicemail PIN: ....

Computer login: ....

Email password: ....

Internet access: ....

Bank card PIN: ....

Family cloud: ....

Back to the Future

Patients with hippocampal damage have more neural problems than just recalling the past or making new memories in the present. In more recent years, studies have found that patients with amnesia caused by hippocampal lesions struggle with creative thinking and conjuring future scenarios. Why, though? Creative thinking demands the rapid recombination of the contents of knowledge and memory to imagine new scenarios. You use the elements available from what you have learned. Without your librarian granting access to these memories, you have little material to work with. That's one reason that this book encourages you to seek novel experiences as fodder for your imagination. Unfortunately, for many patients with severe hippocampal damage, mental time travel into the past or future becomes more difficult or even impossible. They quite literally remain stuck in the present.

Don't Panic!

You might find it nearly or completely impossible to conjure mental images in the creativity or memory tasks. If so, don't panic! It doesn't mean that you have hippocampal damage. If you generally can't form images in your mind's eye, then you may have aphantasia, the inability to create mental imagery. Many aphantasics are born this way, don't know that they lack this ability, and go through life completely normally. They develop other means to recall visual information by translating images into words, showing once again the brain's dynamic and flexible use of different strategies to function successfully and how combining both verbal and visual memory strategies provides you with a more versatile cognitive toolkit.

Now try the creative puzzle on the following page.

4.12 Object-ive Thinking

How many unusual uses do the objects listed below have? Write down as many as you can think of and avoid including anything that the object "normally" does.

fishing net

....

....

....

....

curved door handle

....

....

....

....

....

Who's in the Driver's Seat?

For decades, researchers considered the frontal regions of the brain (right behind your forehead) cognitively "silent" because damage to or removal of tissue in these areas didn't necessarily result in significant losses of a person's mental faculties. But over time, it became apparent that patients with tissue damage in these areas experienced changes in behavior and even personality.

In 1848, railroad worker Phineas Gage experienced a life-changing accident in which an explosion sent an iron rod 43 inches long and 1¼ inches wide upward through his skull, damaging the frontal part of his brain. Astonishingly, right after the injury, Gage stood and walked normally. The doctor who examined him found no cognitive or behavioral abnormalities. However, following the accident, Gage became notably impulsive, often making plans but quickly abandoning them, and engaged in socially inappropriate behavior (boasting, brawling, dishonesty, profanity). He also no longer could hold down a job, even though he had been an excellent employee prior to the accident.

The case of Phineas Gage and many other patients with similar injuries helped neuroscientists learn that these frontal brain regions prove crucial for executive processes, the set of functions we've been calling the "architect" because they support planning actions to achieve a goal while inhibiting unsuitable actions or habits and adapting to new challenges by learning new behaviors. Working memory functions also rely on these regions and their widespread pathways of communication with other brain areas. Similarly, keeping focus to undertake a demanding logical reasoning task also requires these regions to ignore distractions and inhibit urges to give up and relax or do something else. This explains Gage's difficulties to inhibit unsuitable behaviors and stick to his plans.

4.13 Dominoes

Draw along the dashed lines to divide this grid into a complete set of dominoes, from 0-0 to 6-6. Each domino will appear exactly once, so use the cross-off chart to keep track of which dominoes you've placed.

2	5	1	6	3	6	4	4
2	6	6	3	5	6	2	1
0	3	2	3	0	6	2	0
4	4	5	2	1	0	3	4
5	3	1	1	0	1	4	1
2	0	4	3	3	5	6	5
2	6	5	5	1	4	0	0

4.14 Crack the Code

Crack the code used to describe each image and pick which option, 1 to 4, should replace the question mark.

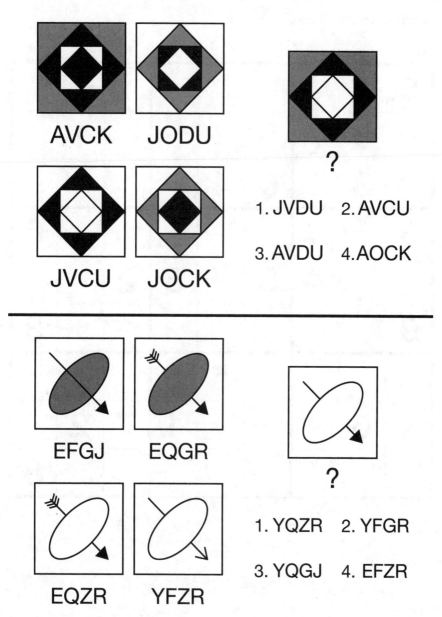

AVCK   JODU

?

1. JVDU   2. AVCU

3. AVDU   4. AOCK

JVCU   JOCK

EFGJ   EQGR

?

1. YQZR   2. YFGR

3. YQGJ   4. EFZR

EQZR   YFZR

4.15 Sudoku

Complete this sudoku puzzle by placing a digit from 1 to 9 into each empty square so that no digit repeats in any row, column, or bold-lined 3×3 box.

5								
	8	7	5				1	
	3		6	4				
8								6
		4	3		5	2		
9								3
				5	3		4	
	6				1	7	2	
								8

Happy Ending

So what happened to poor Phineas Gage in the end? Reports from many years after his accident suggest that he managed to use his remaining frontal lobe regions to adapt slowly to his new circumstances. He even managed to hold down a long-term job working with horses. His story shows us the brain's astonishing potential for recovery and reorganization.

Only the Beginning

Hopefully your journey through this book aided your brain in some healthy reorganization by learning new facts, adapting your thinking, and utilizing new strategies to become a better puzzler. If you made it this far, congratulations on your stamina and willpower! Now keep your momentum going and carry what you've learned into your everyday life.

Try to apply the tips and tricks presented here beyond the confines of these pages. That's the secret to reaping long-term benefits from all your hard work. Your brain will thank you for it.

4.16 What's Missing?

The boxes below contain eight steps in a logical sequence jumbled out of order. One of the boxes is empty, however. Draw the correct picture in it.

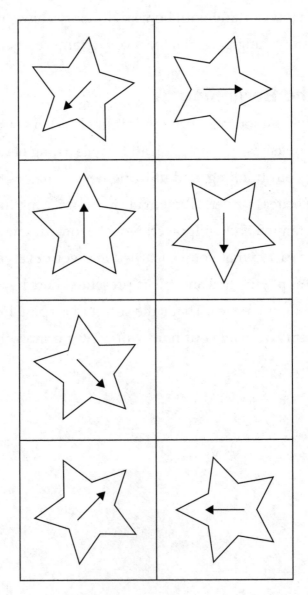

4.17 Careful Counting

How many rectangles and squares of any size appear in the following picture? It contains more than you might think, and don't forget to include the outside shape!

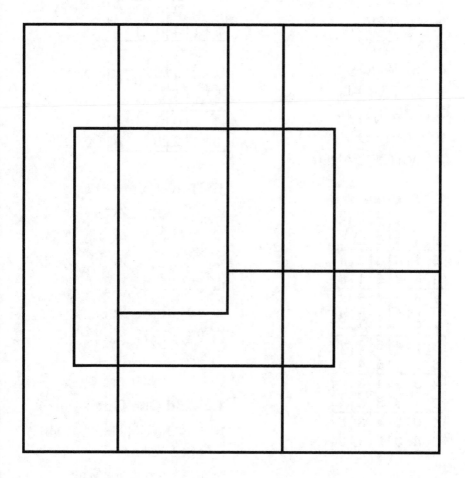

Answer Key

1.2 Country Confusion

▶ PERU
▶ TONGA
▶ ISRAEL
▶ ALGERIA
▶ NORWAY
▶ ECUADOR
▶ PORTUGAL
▶ ARGENTINA
▶ CAMEROON
▶ SWITZERLAND

1.3 Sudoku 6×6

6	3	1	2	4	5
2	5	4	6	3	1
5	1	6	3	2	4
3	4	2	5	1	6
1	6	3	4	5	2
4	2	5	1	6	3

3	5	4	6	2	1
6	2	1	5	4	3
4	3	5	1	6	2
2	1	6	3	5	4
1	6	2	4	3	5
5	4	3	2	1	6

1.4 Dominoes

2	0	4	4	0	4
3	2	1	3	0	2
2	4	1	3	2	2
0	0	3	1	4	0
3	1	4	1	1	3

3	3	2	4	2	2
3	3	1	4	0	0
1	1	2	4	1	4
1	3	0	0	1	4
0	4	2	3	2	0

1.5 Travel Network

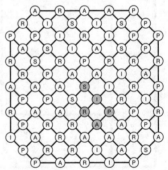

1.6 Odd One Out

▶ E is the only image with 6, not 5, ellipses.

▶ In D, the black/white arrow has its colors flipped relative to the rest.

1.7 Reflect on This

▶ C

▶ D

1.8 Shape Link

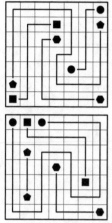

1.9 Top-Down Problem

▶ C

▶ A

1.11 Building Blocks

▶ D

▶ C

1.12 Fold and Punch

▶ B

▶ A

1.13 Password Posers

▶ 1: 3971

▶ 2: diamond

▶ 3: office

▶ 4: 1

▶ 5: 24

▶ 6: bank card PIN

1.15 A Grimm Story

The changes are:

▶ country/citadel

▶ fairies/pixies

▶ fine/ridiculous

▶ many/twenty

▶ grieved/annoyed

▶ gasping/giggling

▶ little/hilarious

▶ river/waterfall

▶ daughter/son

▶ girl/boy

1.19 Number Pyramid

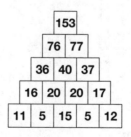

1.21 What's Missing?

A segment is added and the image rotates 90° each step

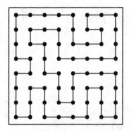

2.3 Shape Link

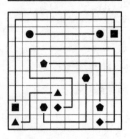

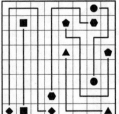

2.4 Fences

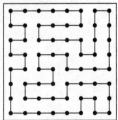

2.5 Hidden Image

▶ C

▶ B

2.6 Tracing Paper

▶ B

▶ D

2.7 Musical Medleys

▶ MADONNA

▶ ELVIS PRESLEY

▶ STEVIE WONDER

▶ ELTON JOHN

▶ ED SHEERAN

▶ TAYLOR SWIFT

▶ DOLLY PARTON

▶ PAUL MCCARTNEY

2.8 A Study in Scarlet

The changes are:

▶ difficult/hard

▶ regular/predictable

▶ breakfasted/eaten

▶ chemical/biology

▶ city/town
▶ seize/grab
▶ sitting/living
▶ vacant/empty

2.9 Shakespearean Shakedown

▶ *As You Like It*
▶ *Much Ado about Nothing*
▶ *A Midsummer Night's Dream*
▶ *The Two Noble Kinsmen*
▶ *The Taming of the Shrew*
▶ *The Two Gentlemen of Verona*
▶ *All's Well That Ends Well*
▶ *The Merry Wives of Windsor*

2.15 Sudoku 9×9

4	1	2	7	6	8	3	9	5
9	7	5	3	2	1	6	8	4
6	3	8	5	9	4	1	2	7
5	4	7	8	3	9	2	6	1
8	6	1	2	4	7	9	5	3
2	9	3	6	1	5	4	7	8
7	2	9	4	8	3	5	1	6
1	5	4	9	7	6	8	3	2
3	8	6	1	5	2	7	4	9

2.16 Number Pyramid

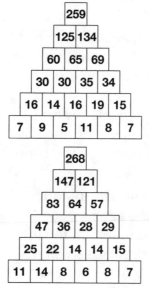

2.17 Crack the Code

▶ c. ZRP
  F = arrow points up
  Z = arrow points down
  Q = large shaded star
  R = large black star
  M = large white star
  K = small star top right
  P = small star bottom left
▶ b. RQX
  W = pointed hexagon top
  R = flat hexagon top
  L = shaded triangle behind
  Q = shaded triangle infront
  X = white background
  H = black background

179

2.18 Complete the Sequence

▶ D. The black circle doesn't move. Moving left to right, a gray bar is added at each stage, with the group of bars moving clockwise around the square edges as the series progresses.

▶ A. Moving left to right along the series, each frame is reflected relative to the previous square, and one new shape is added.

2.19 Complete the Square

▶ A. Each row begins with a small square of a different shade, which rotates 45° in each column moving rightward. A second square is added behind it in the middle column, and then the duo rotates in the rightmost column. Each row and column have exactly one of each shade for the small squares.

▶ C. Arrows point to the grid box with the next higher number of black circles. The circles are arranged randomly around the arrow until a ninth circle covers it.

2.22 Cube Counting

▶ 44 cubes
▶ 35 cubes

2.23 What's Missing?

The black square snakes back and forth, leaving a fading trail. The entire image flips horizontally at each step.

3.2 Olympic Scramble

▶ LUGE
▶ BIATHLON
▶ BADMINTON
▶ ATHLETICS
▶ SKELETON
▶ ROWING
▶ EQUESTRIAN
▶ SNOWBOARDING
▶ SKATEBOARDING

3.3 Recounting Dracula

▶ 1: May 3

▶ 2: 8:35 PM

▶ 3: An hour late

▶ 4: Danube

▶ 5: Hotel Royale

▶ 6: Mina

▶ 7: Carpathians

▶ 8: German

3.5 Odd One Out

▶ C – the only star not overlapped by exactly 6 circles

▶ B – the gray shape has 5 sides, not 4, and the transparent shape has 4 sides, not 5.

3.6 Squaring Up

▶ 14 squares (9 1×1, 4 2×2, and 1 3×3)

▶ 30 squares (16 1×1, 9 2×2, 4 3×3, and 1 4×4)

▶ 55 squares (25 1×1, 16 2×2, 9 3×3, 4 4×4, and 1 5×5)

▶ Sum all square numbers from 1^2 to x^2, inclusive. Mathematically this exercise equates to: $(x(x+1)(2x+1)) \div 6$.

3.7 Building Blocks

▶ C

▶ B

3.8 Cube Counting

▶ 34 cubes

▶ 33 cubes

3.10 Hidden Image

▶ A

▶ D

3.11 Blackout Sudoku

6	1	5	7	9	2	■	8	4
■	9	7	8	6	4	2	1	3
4	2	8	■	5	3	6	7	9
1	5	6	2	4	■	9	3	8
2	8	■	5	3	1	7	4	6
7	4	3	6	8	9	1	5	■
5	■	4	9	2	8	3	6	7
9	3	1	4	7	6	5	■	2
8	7	2	3	■	5	4	9	1

3.12 Number Pyramid

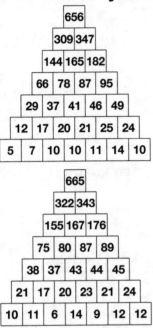

3.13 Jigdoku

D	A	E	B	F	G	C
G	C	B	A	D	E	F
F	E	D	C	G	A	B
E	B	A	G	C	F	D
C	D	G	F	E	B	A
B	F	C	E	A	D	G
A	G	F	D	B	C	E

3.14 What's Missing?

At each step, an extra circle is added to the perimeter, one corner clockwise from the previously added circle. When a second circle is added to an existing one, a larger

transparent circle is added on top. In addition, the entire image rotates 45° clockwise, and the two ellipses change their stacking order back and forth at each step.

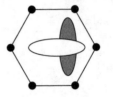

3.15 Complete the Sequence

▶ D. A new central pointer shape is added at each stage, reading from left to right. Each new shape is shaded darker than the previous added shape and laid on top. Small black dots appear in the space pointed to by the shape added in the previous frame. An arrow is added along the bottom of each frame, alternating between bottom right and bottom left placement.

▶ E. Reading from left to right across the frames, a new set of eight "arrows" is added at each stage, each increasing in size and pointing out from the center of the arrangement. The style of arrow added at each stage is included in the corner of each frame, pointing to a different corner each time and moving clockwise around the frame.

3.16 Complete the Square

▶ D. The total number of points on all the stars in each row and column adds to 15. Also, stars with even numbers of points have a hatched background.

▶ C. A black rectangle is overlaid at 90° atop a gray rectangle across the 9 squares, with four circular cut-out holes on the four central grid intersections. Also, every even-numbered square (reading left to right, top to bottom from 1 at the top-left) has been flipped horizontally. Without this flipping, the completed grid would look like this:

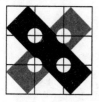

3.21 Shape Link

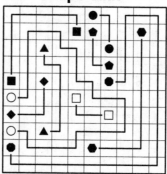

3.22 Tracing Paper

▶ B
▶ C

3.23 Careful Counting

36

4.1 Top-Down Problem

▶ B
▶ D

4.2 Reflect on This

▶ A
▶ B

4.3 Shape Link

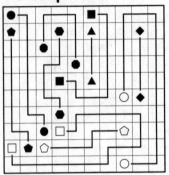

4.4 Fences

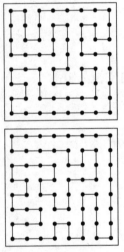

4.5 Fold and Punch

▶ A
▶ D

4.8 Fruity Finding

▶ DATE
▶ LIME
▶ MANGO
▶ APRICOT
▶ PINEAPPLE
▶ TAMARIND
▶ NECTARINE
▶ ELDERBERRY
▶ POMEGRANATE

4.10 Poor Little Women

The changes are:

▶ presents/gifts
▶ rug/carpet
▶ dreadful/awful
▶ dress/skirt
▶ pretty/lovely
▶ injured/unhappy
▶ contentedly/reassuringly
▶ young/youthful
▶ darkened/fell
▶ fighting/war

4.13 Dominoes

2	5	1	6	3	6	4	4
2	6	6	3	5	6	2	1
0	3	2	3	0	6	2	0
4	4	5	2	1	0	3	4
5	3	1	1	0	1	4	1
2	0	4	3	3	5	6	5
2	6	5	5	1	4	0	0

4.14 Crack the Code

▶ b. AVCU

A = large gray square
J = large white square
O = large gray diamond
V = large black diamond
C = small white square
D = small black square
K = small black diamon
U = small white diamond

▶ d. EFZR

E = solid arrowhead
Y = non-solid arrowhead
Q = tail feathers
F = no tail feathers
G = gray oval
Z = white oval
R = oval in front
J = oval behind

4.15 Sudoku

5	4	9	1	3	7	8	6	2
6	8	7	5	2	9	3	1	4
2	3	1	6	4	8	5	9	7
8	5	3	9	1	2	4	7	6
1	7	4	3	6	5	2	8	9
9	2	6	7	8	4	1	5	3
7	9	2	8	5	3	6	4	1
3	6	8	4	9	1	7	2	5
4	1	5	2	7	6	9	3	8

4.16 What's Missing?

At each step, the entire image rotates 45° clockwise.

4.17 Careful Counting

28

Progress Notes

Use these pages to track your progress.

Progress Notes

Progress Notes

Track Your Points

Each time you try a puzzle, write a score in the POINTS box at the top of that puzzle or page.

Give yourself 5 points if you tried a puzzle and 10 points if you successfully completed a puzzle. For puzzles without specific solutions, such as creativity tasks, give yourself 10 points for giving it a good try. For memory tasks, give yourself 10 points if you did your best. Or, in both cases, 5 points for "could try harder."

Track your chapter totals below, then, when you have worked through the entire book, total your overall points.

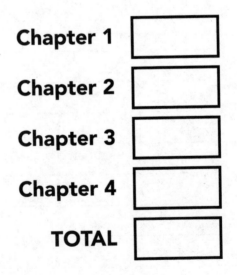

Chapter 1

Chapter 2

Chapter 3

Chapter 4

TOTAL

About the Authors

Gareth Moore, PhD, is the best-selling author of more than 250 brain-training and puzzle books for children and adults. Published in more than 30 languages, his books have sold more than 5 million copies worldwide. A former board member of the World Puzzle Federation, he serves as a director of the UK Puzzle Association. He created the brain-training site BrainedUp.com and runs the daily puzzle site PuzzleMix.com. He lives in London. Visit him online at DrGarethMoore.com.

Helena Gellersen, PhD, earned her doctorate in psychology from the University of Cambridge, studying the cognitive neuroscience of memory in aging. She holds a postdoctoral position at the German Center for Neurodegenerative Diseases, researching brain changes in people with preclinical Alzheimer's disease and developing novel memory tasks to enable early detection. Her research has appeared in numerous peer-reviewed journals, podcasts, and blogs. With Gareth Moore, she cowrote *Memory Palace Master,* in which she explains the cognitive neuroscience of memory and mnemonic strategies. She lives in Göttingen, Germany.

For information about permission to reproduce selections from this book, write to Permissions, Countryman Press, 500 Fifth Avenue, New York, NY 10110

For information about special discounts for bulk purchases, please contact W. W. Norton Special Sales at specialsales@wwnorton.com or 800-233-4830

Manufacturing by Lakeside Book Company

Library of Congress Control Number: 2023946373

Countryman Press
www.countrymanpress.com

An imprint of W. W. Norton & Company, Inc.
500 Fifth Avenue, New York, NY 10110
www.wwnorton.com

978-1-68268-877-9 (pbk)

1 2 3 4 5 6 7 8 9 0